Once in a great while someone has the courage to write an honest book about real faith colliding with real life.

I read it in one day because I couldn't put it down. From the first chapter, *When Hope Met Hopelessness* is a true-life story of love and tragedy. Heartbreak and generosity. Hope and hopelessness. Fear and trust. Faith and loss.

With startling honesty, Jeanne writes, "I don't even know what day it is . . . My days stopped when my Crystal died." Her book then helps the reader answer questions like: *Where is God when my world implodes? How could God let tragedy happen?*

And then, with startling wisdom, Jeanne moves the reader forward with questions like: *How do you make your darkest hours your defining moment? What can you count on when you can't count on anything?*

Ultimately, the reader is left with one thought—Maybe God is at work even in moments when it looks like God is absent.

For those of us needing encouragement and hope (and who isn't?), this book is a Godsend! Buy it. Read it. And give one to the people you love.

—Ray Johnson, founding pastor of Bayside Church, author

When Hope Met Hopelessness is a powerful testimony to the work of God in our lives amidst tragedy and suffering. Jeanne Rodriguez writes authentically and with vulnerability about how God can take our places of hopelessness and infuse them with divine hope. A must read for anyone who has experienced grief and loss, and for those who have come alongside others in their hardships.

—Rev. Dr. Libby Vincent, Episcopal priest and spiritual director

If we ever needed hope, it's now. This is not just another book—it's one woman's story of loss, struggle and finding hope again. Jeanne's path of daring to trust God after loss is compelling. I found myself unable to stop reading. This book reminded me that God can be trusted and found faithful even amidst the disappointment of shattered dreams and especially in God's own orchestration of new beginnings.

—Debbie Alsdorf, author of *Deeper, The Faith Dare*, and *It's Momplicated*

I usually read fast, but while reading *When Hope Met Hopelessness*, I felt both the desire and need to slow and be immersed in a true story and moment. It is impossible to move to hope without moving through the neighborhood of brokenness. Jeanne and Ruben Rodriguez model the journey daily. *When Hope Met Hopelessness* is an invitation to hope, regardless of what has assailed your ability to hope. Say yes to this invitation!

—Leonard Lee, DDC, director of the 4GENetwork, Author of *Leading from the Middle: How the Leadership of Jesus Launched a Movement*

I hope that you take the time to read this heartwarming story of great tragedy and the struggle to return to normal. This will clearly help many but will also give perspective to some. Grief comes unwelcomed, but when it arrives, it must be entertained and hosted because it will be with you for a long while. Many kudos to Jeanne and her husband for the journey they went on and the charm in which they have shared this powerful story.

—Dr. Gil Stieglitz, founder and president of Principles To Live By (PTLB), Author, speaker, pastor

In *When Hope Met Hopelessness*, we get a glimpse into the kind of nightmare that devastates the very depths of a mother's heart. In this raw and authentic story, we go on a journey with Jeanne from bliss to shock to grief to hopelessness. In that devastation we see her strength rise when God is present, providing loving comfort and correction. It is moving; it is real. I recommend you read with tissues . . . lots of tissues.

—Victoria M. Newman, founder and president of How2LoveOurCops

For anyone who has experienced a great loss or is walking alongside someone who has, this book will deeply touch and inspire you. As you follow Jeanne's raw, heartfelt, and authentic journey, you will find glimmers of hope and glimpses of joy—handholds needed to find healing. This is no lightweight placebo or band-aid—it overflows with gut-wrenching honesty as Jeanne shares how she has worked through the layers of grief, her determination to not let anger rule, and her openness to God in the midst of devastation. From the depths of her story of tragedy and anguish, Jeanne infuses the reader with great hope and inspiration.

—Dee Bright, author of *The Divine Romance—Going to God with the Longings Only He Can Fulfill when*

HOPE

met hopelessness

To Diane —

May the Lord bless you
and keep you. May He be gracious
and kind and may His face
shine on you.

You are loved!

In Christ alone —

Jeanne

numbers 6: 24-26

when

HOPE

met hopelessness

A T R U E S T O R Y

JEANNE RODRIGUEZ
foreword by Nicole Johnson

REDEMPTION
PRESS

Published by Redemption Press, PO Box 427, Enumclaw, WA 98022.
Toll-Free (844) 2REDEEM (273-3336)

Redemption Press is honored to present this title in partnership with the author. The views expressed or implied in this work are those of the author. Redemption Press provides our imprint seal representing design excellence, creative content, and high-quality production.

The author has tried to recreate events, locales, and conversations from memories of them. In order to maintain their anonymity, in some instances the names of individuals, some identifying characteristics, and some details may have been changed, such as physical properties, occupations, and places of residence.

ISBN 13: 978-1-64645-599-7 (Paperback)
978-1-64645-598-0 (ePub)
978-1-64645-597-3 (Mobi)

Library of Congress Catalog Card Number: 2022904067

DEDICATION

Dedicated to Victor—If only you could read my heart, then you would surely know how much I love you and how proud I am of you! You walked through this journey and never became bitter. Your faithfulness to God during this catastrophic time in your life is an example and inspiration to me.

Dedicated to Crystal—You have left us with a wonderful legacy. It has been only on rare occasions that someone so "young" has left such an impact on my life. I fell in love with your personality and your heart. Your love for life, for the Lord and for Victor was simply incredible.

You never said I'm leaving,
You never said goodbye.
You were gone before I knew it,
And only God knew why.
A million times I needed you,
A million times I cried,
If love alone could have saved you,
You never would have died.
In life I loved you dearly,
In death I love you still.
In my heart you hold a place,
That no one could ever fill.
It broke my heart to lose you,
But you didn't go alone.
For part of me went with you,
The day God took you home.[1]
—Author Unknown

TABLE OF CONTENTS

FOREWORD

I REMEMBER THE EVENING I met Jeanne Rodriguez in Roseville, California. She was only a year or so past the tragedy that unfolds here in her book. She waited patiently until others were gone to speak with me privately.

The minute our eyes met I could see her anguish. Suffering marks us. It changes something in our eyes that often only others who have suffered can see. It is as though we've been forced into a club we never wanted to join. But when we discover other "members" of this club, or they discover us, bonds are created faster than superglue and deeper than the roots of an oak tree.

As the details, questions, and pain of her story tumbled out in inadequate words, my heart broke for Jeanne. Yours will too. What she endured was too much, too sad, and too difficult, for her tender heart and yet, what choice do any of us ever have when it comes to suffering? A simple, "No thank you, I'll pass." What an affront to our faith.

Jeanne writes as she loves, authentically and simply. She is not a flowery, adjective heavy Christian, she is a serving, loving, sacrificing, wife and mother and her book is as honest as her life. My friend's questions are hard, but they are good questions, and rightly given the weight they deserve in her story. Would that more writers would choose to "open a vein and put their blood on the page."

If you've ever felt you would never stop crying, if your loss has ever felt more than you could bear, read on; you'll find a sister in these pages. Let Jeanne be your guide, your companion to walk with in grief; before you try to walk through grief. In time, you will come out on the other side, but Jeanne will not let you race to get there. In following her lead, and in her footsteps, you too can experience what happens when hopelessness meets its match.

—Nicole Johnson, Author, Dramatist,
Speaker, Creator of Seasons Weekend

PREFACE

THIS IS THE STORY of the life and death of my sweet daughter-in-law. She was only my daughter-in-law for twelve days, but she was a part of our family from the first day we met her. I wrote this book for several reasons, a large part of which was to share my journey of grief and healing in the hopes that it will speak to others.

For those who've lost a loved one, I want you to know that it's okay to grieve. It's a process that lingers and you can't speed it up no matter how much you try. Sit in it for however long it takes. And know that it's okay to cry; you don't have to apologize for it! I also want you to know that it's okay to be angry with God. He's big enough and strong enough. He can handle it! But know that He's always with you, even when you're angry with Him.

For those who've never had a major loss in your lives, I hope this story and my words will help you have a better understanding of what your family and friends may be experiencing in their loss.

Ultimately, my desire is that this book will bring hope. As the title says, "When Hope Met Hopelessness." I was truly hopeless in the midst of our devastating loss and through God's grace and timing, I've rediscovered His hope. I want you to know that eventually your pain will dull. One day, you too will find yourself smiling as you think of a sweet memory of years past. And whether you're currently smiling or still sobbing, God is there with you. He hears your cries and invites you to lean into Him for comfort.

Thank you so much for taking the time to read my story.

With Love and Gratitude,
Jeanne Rodriguez

Chapter One

THE WEDDING

And How We Got Here . . .

*Love does not consist of gazing at each other, but in looking
outward together in the same direction.*

—Antoine de Saint-Exupery[2]

"TODAY I'M GETTING MARRIED!" Crystal exclaimed as she
bounded into Penny's picturesque home in the Northern California
foothills. She had been looking forward to this day for eleven months.
It was finally here! Albeit with rain . . . pouring rain . . . Who would
have thought there'd be rain in June? Certainly not Crystal! But the
wet weather wasn't going to dampen her excitement and joy for the
day ahead. Though we didn't sense it at the time, it would seem that
the rain foreshadowed what was to come. Were those possibly heaven's
tears for Victor and Crystal?

I'm getting ahead of myself. Let me first tell you how we got here . . .

Victor and Crystal were thrilled when our friends Tim and Penny
Doane offered their property for their wedding venue. The beautifully
landscaped acreage was adorned by an array of flowers in so many
varieties and colors, tall oak trees, an oval shaped pond and even a
waterfall; all lovingly tended to for this special occasion.

It was finally here . . . the week of the wedding! But it really didn't
look like the weather was going to cooperate. On Tuesday, I spent the

whole day anxiously calling locations to see if they were available in case we were rained out. Venues, those we could afford and those we couldn't, were all filled. Now what?

In my panic, I prayed. I really didn't want to stress out Crystal, so I kept my concerns to myself for the day. The next afternoon, Pastor Rob Maxey called me. He was officiating and he too had concerns. "I hate to sound negative, but do you have a Plan B for Saturday?" Before I could respond, he continued, "Our church would like to offer our [large] sanctuary for the wedding ceremony and reception."

What an answer to prayer! Their church was booked every weekend surrounding the wedding, including the entire month of June. I asked Pastor Rob if we could take a look before making a decision. Not long after we spoke, my sister Mary and I headed to the church. As we looked around, we knew it would be perfect. The room could easily hold 250 people for the ceremony and sit-down dinner reception. We unofficially decided that was our backup plan.

Thursday morning my husband, Rubén, came downstairs with a printed copy of the weather report. He handed it to me and said, "Seventy-one percent chance of rain; I don't think there's going to be an outdoor wedding." Reluctantly, I called Crystal. The rainy weather report for Saturday and the generous offer from the pastor was met with, "Do you *really* think it's going to rain on Saturday?" While I told her what I really thought, I also indicated that she needed to be the one to make the final decision. She said she'd have to get back to me.

I recognized that Crystal needed to make the decision and I didn't want to tell her what to do, but I also knew we didn't have time to wait. That morning, the linens, plates, and glassware were scheduled to be delivered to the wedding site and I couldn't postpone it. Though Crystal had to make the call, I knew deep down that we wouldn't be having an outdoor wedding. So, without telling her, I had everything delivered to the church. I knew it was the right call, but I was worried all day long hoping Crystal would come to the same conclusion. I called her several more times anxiously awaiting her reply.

Finally, around five o'clock, she called to tell me they would have the wedding at the church. Whew, was I relieved!

The next two days were a whirlwind of activities. Topping the list was notifying 250 people of the location change, reconfiguring the guest seating to account for the different size tables, and decorating the sanctuary.

On the morning of the wedding, I watched as all our friends rallied together to make the inside of the church beautiful. As we got started, my co-worker Nancy Deglymes asked, "Jeanne, what are your plans for the foyer?" With a glazed and slightly panicked look on my face, I exclaimed, "There wasn't a foyer when we planned the wedding!" Nancy instantly responded, "Would you like me to bring some calla lilies from my home?" Overwhelmed with gratitude, I replied with an emphatic, "Yes!" She drove a half-hour back to her house, put on some mukluks, gathered enough calla lilies to fill the foyer and returned with such beautiful arrangements. It looked absolutely stunning!

While my friends and I were preparing the church, the wedding party was getting ready at Tim and Penny's house. The bridesmaids wore teal and black, the color of Victor's favorite hockey team, the San Jose Sharks. Crystal wasn't going to let the rain get her down, so she had brainstormed with her friend and photographer Tori Wible, and they decided to get everyone rainboots and umbrellas. Tori captured beautiful pictures of the bride, groom, and bridal party playing outside in the rain. Then, for a little escape from the elements, Tori took them to Bushnell Gardens for additional wedding party photos.

Plan A or Plan B, it didn't matter. The wedding was beyond anything I could have imagined! Watching my son's face—eyes glistening and an ear-to-ear smile as his lingering glance followed Crystal down the aisle—was priceless. And I was filled with just as much joy as I turned to look at Crystal . . . this incredible young woman whose smile exuded such love for him. This was the day we had been looking forward to. The past four years led to this very day . . . this moment . . . when Crystal was officially going to be our daughter.

Long before the wedding, Crystal became the daughter we never had. We truly loved her as if she were our own. In the years leading up to their engagement, Crystal spent almost every day with us doing her college homework at our home. She joined us for family dinners, went on vacations with us, and even joined us for family portraits before we knew Victor was going to propose.

Fast forward three years . . . Rubén and I had known for some time that Victor was going to ask Crystal to marry him. In fact, I remember when Victor asked me to go with him to get her ring. He knew the ring he wanted but needed a little help. Victor said, "Dad told me you're really good at negotiating prices. Will you come?" So, along we went. Victor picked out the engagement ring and matching wedding band and I negotiated a great price. He was overly impressed with his Momma.

Just two months later, over the fourth of July weekend, Victor and Crystal were going camping at Dillon Beach with their best friends. Victor had it all planned out, he was going to propose to Crystal on the fourth. On July third, I received a text that said, "She said YES!" Shortly after, he called. While I was thrilled, and told him just how happy I was, I asked, "I thought you were going to propose on the fourth?" I could hear the smile in his voice as he replied, "I couldn't wait, Mom." We laughed; then Crystal got on the phone, and we talked for a bit. I really don't know who was more excited, her or me!

Crystal was extremely close to her Grandma Donna and, unfortunately, not long after the engagement, Crystal learned that her grandma had been diagnosed with liver cancer. Donna had raised Crystal since she was in the fifth grade. There's a lot that I won't get into, but basically Crystal wanted and needed consistency in her life and neither of her parents could give that to her. Donna gladly stepped in and loved every moment of it! Shortly after Victor proposed, Donna and I went with Crystal to choose her wedding dress. Sadly, Donna would never get to see her walk down the aisle in it, as she died in January 2011, just five months before the wedding.

I was blessed and honored to help Crystal with some of the more girly wedding tasks, like officially ordering the dress that she and Donna had chosen, picking out invitations, and selecting flowers. I was also there with Victor and Crystal as they made their invite lists, picked the food for the reception, and chose their photographer and DJ. At one point Victor said, "Mom, you're like the mother of the groom and the mother of the bride!" I happily replied, "Yes, yes I am, and I love every minute of it!!"

In the midst of all the planning, I remember someone asking me what the theme was for their wedding. I panicked. Theme? It's a wedding; isn't that the theme? I didn't know you were supposed to have a *theme*. I'm terrible with coming up with stuff like that, so I called Crystal and asked, "What's the theme of the wedding?" She replied, "I guess if we were to have a theme, it would be 'fun.'" That's what she wanted for everyone—to have fun, to dance, to laugh, and to celebrate with them.

Even though it was pouring outside, Crystal got her dream wedding with the man she loved with all her heart. Throughout the night, I watched them as they laughed, kissed, danced, and just had lots and lots of fun! I could replay the whole day for you . . . every single detail. Instead, I'll share just a couple of my favorite moments . . .

After Victor and Crystal cut the cake, they had their first dance, a traditional slow dance to "When You Say Nothing at All."[3] It was beautiful. Then, part way through, the song mixed into several others. It was a slow dance turned dance party. Really, I shouldn't have expected anything else! Victor and Crystal each took turns dancing to different styles of music. Everyone there laughed and cheered alongside the bride and groom. And just as quickly as it had ramped up, the music slowed back down, Victor and Crystal returned to an intimate dance, and they finished with a kiss. It was such a fun first dance and the perfect representation of the two of them.

Another one of my favorites was the mother-son dance; it was pure happiness! We took the moment to talk about how incredible the day had turned out. Victor thanked me for everything I did for their wedding, and I told him just how proud I was of him and ecstatic for the two of them. I laughed and cried and took in the moment as we swayed to Celine Dion's, "Because You Loved Me."[4]

The dance floor was still crowded as the DJ played the last song of the evening. Six hours went by so quickly; it really was such a fun wedding! When the song finished, the guests lined the walkway outside and made a stunning arch of sparklers. Off they ran, Victor and Crystal ducking under the spray of sparkling lights.

Chapter Two

THE HONEYMOON
And What Shouldn't Have Been

I see trees of green, red roses, too.
I see them bloom, for me and you.
And I think to myself.
What a wonderful world!

—Louis Armstrong5

VICTOR AND CRYSTAL LOVED family, so instead of whisking off on their honeymoon, they spent the next day with family. Between the two of them, we had family members who flew in from New Jersey, New York, Maryland, Arizona, and Southern California. So, in the morning, Victor and Crystal had breakfast with us and in the afternoon, they had a barbeque with Crystal's family. Later in the evening, they came back to our house to open their wedding gifts.

That evening, Crystal told Rubén and me that she and Victor were going out to breakfast with her Grandma Sherry and Grandpa Jim. Her grandparents had driven up from Arizona and she wanted to spend the last morning with them before heading off for their honeymoon. Over the years, Crystal had shared so many memorable stories about them and we finally met them for the first time at the rehearsal dinner. Crystal wanted us to join them for breakfast so we could get to know them even better.

It was wonderful spending that time with the kids and Crystal's grandparents. It was such a delight to listen as they reminisced. Even though we already knew some stories, it was fun listening to Jim and Sherry tell them as they remembered. They were so proud of their granddaughter, and I could see how much she loved them. The time flew by so quickly and before we knew it, it was time to say goodbye to her grandparents.

That afternoon, Rubén was taking not only Crystal and Victor to the airport, but also my nephews who had flown in from New Jersey. I had originally planned to see Victor and Crystal off at the airport, but when I went out to the van, it was packed with suitcases and there wasn't an inch of room. I said my goodbyes to everyone and told the kids I'd see them when they got back home. I sent them off with a wave as Rubén drove away.

First stop: Southern California! My oldest son Kevin gave Victor and Crystal two tickets to Disneyland as a wedding gift, and they added a day at Universal Studios to the mix. After that, they were headed to the beach in the Bahamas to stay in one of our timeshares.

I took the following week off from work after the wedding and was back to work on Monday, June 13th. That Thursday was June 16, 2011—the day before Victor and Crystal were due back from their honeymoon. The date is permanently stamped in my mind forever and you'll soon discover why. It was a productive day, but it was also the first day implementing a new team protocol. Basically, my phone was to remain off and in my purse except for lunch. I checked my phone at lunch, and I hadn't received any calls. I left the office a little after four o'clock and headed straight to the grocery store to pick up a few items for my Friday Bible Study's mini retreat. We were kicking things off at five o'clock, so I didn't have a lot of time. As I parked, I looked at my phone and noticed that I had two missed calls from an out-of-town number. The calls came in right after lunch, but I hadn't noticed them until now.

As I listened, the message just didn't make sense. The man on the other end said his name was Officer Joe from Customs and Borders

Protection. My mind started racing as I heard Victor's name and I thought, "What did the kids get themselves into?" Directly followed by, "I didn't even know the Bahamas had a border." But suddenly, I heard "accident" and "Victor's all right." I didn't even listen to the second message. I immediately called Joe back.

As it turned out, Joe was on vacation in the Bahamas from Michigan where he worked with the U.S. Customs and Borders Protection. He's also an EMT and had helped Victor. As Joe told it, Victor and Crystal were parasailing and there was an accident causing the kids to fall into the water. Crystal was pulled in first and Joe started doing CPR. A nurse came over to help and Joe moved over to Victor to check him over. Crystal was beside Victor on the beach, and while they waited for the ambulance to arrive, Joe told me that he took Crystal's hand and put it into Victor's.

He told me that Victor had a chest tube put in and he thought he was okay. Joe gave me the name of the hospital and the number, but he also gave me a Detective Johnson's number and said to call him first. He said that it was a small hospital, and they may not be as helpful.

I was completely overwhelmed by everything I had just heard and a little perplexed that he wanted me to call a detective, but I was in too much of a rush to find out why. So, I called Detective Johnson. As he gave me the rundown, he said, "Victor is in the ICU and, to my knowledge, is in stable condition." He also told me that they were investigating into the cause of the accident.

Since he hadn't said anything about Crystal, I asked how she was doing. I pictured her worried and all alone while Victor was in the ICU. What's so crazy is that I had already been told that Crystal was pulled in from the water, but it never occurred to me that she was hurt even though Joe told me he did CPR. The detective asked, "You haven't gotten a call?" I knew right then by the sound of his voice that something serious had happened.

"Is she okay?" I asked. He didn't answer.

My voice rose an octave and I shouted, "Is she dead?" There was silence on the other end.

After a moment, he said that he needed to talk to her family. I replied, "I *am* her family!" He clarified, "I need to talk to her mom or dad." To which I replied, "Crystal's grandma raised her, and she died in January." He then asked me if I knew where her mom and dad were. I was getting anxious, annoyed, and frightened. My response was quite terse, "I have no idea where they are! I'm the mom to Crystal and I need you to tell me what happened!"

By this point, I was frantic and practically yelling at the detective. He replied, "Ma'am, I won't be able to speak with you in the state that you're in. I need you to calm down." I took a deep breath and as I was doing so, I asked the Lord to calm me down. By the time I exhaled, I felt a peace within me. I very calmly said, "I'm really okay. I just need to ask a few questions." He agreed. I then again asked him how Crystal was doing. He told me Crystal's injuries were more serious than Victor's. I then asked him if she was in the ICU. His answer was no. I then directly asked him, "Did she die?"

He carefully chose his words and once again repeated, "Crystal's injuries were more grievous than Victor's." I told him that in the United States the ICU takes on the most serious cases and then I asked, "In the Bahamas, do you have another unit other than the ICU that handles the most serious cases?" The detective said that they didn't. Then I said, "So, if Victor is in the ICU and Crystal isn't in the ICU and her injuries were more grievous than Victor's, then she must have died." At that point, he said "Yes." I thanked him for talking with me and telling me what happened and hung up.

I immediately called Rubén. He was still at work. I was still calm as I started telling him what happened. But when it came time to tell him that Crystal was dead, I fell apart. I started screaming, "She died. She died! She's dead!" and Rubén just kept saying, "NO, NO, she can't have died!!"

Rubén finally said, "I'm leaving work right away! You should come home. Where are you?" I told him that I was in front of Safeway. "I don't want you to drive, Jeanne," he said. "I'll call Joanna," I replied. As it turned out, Joanna was down the street at Mary's house (that's where the mini retreat was being held). Without missing a beat, Joanna said, "I'm coming straight over to be with you."

While I waited, I called my sister and we both sobbed as I told her what happened. "Mary, I need you to call the rest of the family . . . Mom and our three brothers . . . I emotionally just can't say it again." Mary said she'd do whatever I needed and let me know she was there for us in the midst of all of this.

My friend, Joanna Larrew and Theresa Maloney showed up and I wept on Joanna's shoulder as she just held me. After I don't know how long, I finally got myself together enough to climb into Joanna's car and Theresa drove my car back to the house. The ride is a blur. I just remember sitting there sobbing uncontrollably. I couldn't wrap my head around the fact that Crystal had died. How can that be? They were on their honeymoon—who dies on their honeymoon?! She was only twenty-two years old—they were so in love—they were the perfect pair! In a matter of twelve days, our family went from the happiest moment in our lives to the very darkest days. How could this happen?! How can this be?! I don't understand. I must have voiced something out loud because Joanna replied, "There are some things we will never understand." How true was that statement?

Rubén arrived home at the same time as I did. We just hugged and cried together in the driveway. But we couldn't stand there forever, calls had to be made. I didn't have it in me and so I told him that he needed to make them. Rubén, broken over this loss too, went upstairs to call Crystal's dad and mom and to make a few calls to his own family as well.

Chapter Three

THE BAHAMAS

When Can We Get Out of Here?

Death leaves a heartache no one can heal. Love leaves a memory no one can steal.

—(Carved on a headstone in Ireland)

RUBÉN KNEW THAT WE would need not only moral support down in the Bahamas, but someone who could think clearly. He immediately called his brother Manny, who lives in New York, and asked him if he would join us in the Bahamas. Manny, being the incredible brother (and brother-in-law) that he is, said yes without hesitation.

As Rubén continued to make calls notifying our family and friends, my phone started ringing off the hook. I simply couldn't handle talking to people, so I turned my phone over to Joanna. Then, friends started showing up at our house. The first one who came by was a long-time friend, Donna Gonzalez. She came in, gave me a long, long hug, and proceeded to put a wad of money in my hand. "It's to help you as you travel to the Bahamas," she whispered in my ear. I was so out of my mind with grief that I didn't even think of inviting her to stay. Honestly, I still regret that.

It seemed right after Donna left that other friends started show-ing up . . . hugging, kissing, crying . . . They stayed. Every one of them. Our living room just started filling up with our dear friends. At one point, I looked up and saw Joanna, phone to her ear, motioning for someone to stop. Curiosity got the best of me, and I went over to see what was going on. There, on the lawn, were all six of Victor's groomsmen from the wedding party. Honestly, I don't even know how everyone found out so quickly, but we had such a huge support system! Overcome with emotions, tears filled my eyes as I walked toward them. Victor's best man grabbed me, hugged me, and started praying for me. He said that they wanted us to know that all the groomsmen were praying and that they were here for us.

Ray Johnston, my pastor, got the news and called me. "I heard what happened, Jeanne. I want you to know that my assistant is going to take care of getting airline tickets for you and Rubén. We'll take care of anything you need!" On top of that, they arranged to bring my son Kevin up from Huntington Beach.

Kevin was remarkably close to Crystal. She was like a sister to him, and he'd talked to her almost daily. Even though Kevin wasn't going to the Bahamas with us, we knew that he would need to be surrounded by his lifelong friends as he dealt with Crystal's death. The earliest flight we could get for him was six in the morning. As we talked through everything with him, we suggested, "Just call a taxi in the morning to take you to the airport. Okay, Kevin?" He was so distraught that he didn't even have it within him to do that. See, Kevin has Asperger Syndrome and stressful things can overwhelm him. You can't get more stressful than to lose someone you love.

As Rubén and I were trying to figure out what to do about the situation, my dear friend Cathy Haviland walked over and asked where our computer was located. Not thinking anything of it, I told her it was upstairs and off she went. Rubén and I were still talking when Cathy came back down. "I'm off to the airport," she said. We looked perplexed. That's when she told us that she had gone upstairs to book the last flight to Los Angeles so that she could pick Kevin up and take him to the airport in the morning. I was overcome by her love for my son and her love for our family.

The Lord was definitely watching over Kevin. Not only was Cathy going down to get him, but it turned out that a friend of our family was at Disneyland that day. Later that evening, she and her husband drove to Kevin's place and spent the evening with him.

Shortly after Cathy left, our dear friends and neighbors Mike and Linda Glynn came over. Mike went inside and Linda and I sat on the swing out front. We sat there a bit and she began to share how much she loved the kids. "Jeanne, it just brought me so much joy to be able to help them wash all the new dishes and glasses they received at Crystal's bridal shower." It was a small moment, but those are often some of the sweetest. As we sat and talked, I saw Pastor Rob walking up our driveway. I slowly got up and moved toward him, and as I did, tears started flowing down my cheeks. I sobbed, "Rob, you married them twelve days ago and now you will be burying her." He gathered Rubén, me, and all our friends and prayed over us. He prayed a lot of things but what I remember is that he prayed for Victor and for the Lord to comfort us all during our time of need.

As we continued to make arrangements for our time in the Bahamas, I was told that our church wasn't only planning on taking care of our plane tickets but our hotel, too. As it turned out, Taino Beach Resort where we sent Victor and Crystal on their honeymoon said they would put us up free of charge while we were there. So many provisions were being met in our time of greatest need!

With friends gathered around us, Rubén called the hospital to see if we could speak to Victor. They abruptly told us to call back. I realized just how small the hospital was the second time Rubén called because Victor's doctor answered the phone. Rubén put the doctor on speakerphone and that's when we found out the extent of Victor's injuries. He had six broken ribs, a laceration on his liver and one on his spleen, and his lung was punctured so he had a tube in his chest. We then asked the doctor if Victor knew of Crystal's death. He replied, "We just told him." The doctor then held the phone to Victor's ear, and we told him how very sorry we were. There's nothing more hopeless than comforting your son in the loss of his new wife over the phone thousands of miles apart.

Victor asked us when we were coming. "Just as soon as we can, Son," we told him. Then, with immense sorrow in his voice, he said, "Mom, Crystal's dead and I'm all alone. I need you and Dad to be here." We cried as we told him we were coming as fast as we could. After Rubén hung up, I started to pray quietly, asking the Lord to take care of my son who was all alone. I asked that Victor would sense His presence and His love and that he wouldn't feel so alone.

Rubén and I were in a fog as we were trying to process all that happened and all that needed to be done. Fortunately, our friends were thinking ahead. They knew we needed clothes and, of course, most of our clothes were in the laundry basket. Our neighbor and friend, Jackie Batchelor, took the dark clothes over to her house to wash and dry as Joanna did a load of whites at our house.

Amid all the planning, we realized that Rubén didn't have a regular passport. He always had a military passport and never changed it over when he retired from the Air National Guard. So, on top of everything else, our pastor's assistant had to keep that in mind as she was getting our tickets to fly to the Bahamas. We knew we would have to go to San Francisco to get a passport before we could fly out the next morning.

Several hours after we found out about the accident, I received a call from the American Ambassador in the Bahamas who informed us of Crystal's death. I told him that we were aware of everything that happened. Next, he asked, "Is there anything that we can do for you?" Without even thinking, I responded, "My husband needs a passport." "We'll take care of it," he told me. "Check in at the passport office, they will be waiting for you."

That night, Rubén posted the following message on Facebook:

Today is a tragic day for two families, recently joined as one. Most of you already know that Victor and Crystal were involved in a terrible sporting accident in the Bahamas on the last day of their honeymoon, one day before coming home to begin their new life together. Victor is seriously hurt and remains in the ICU, but our dear new daughter-in-law Crystal passed away due to the extent of her injuries.

Words will never be able to express this loss. We only had her in our lives for a brief four years, but they were years in which she changed us. She made us better as a family. I, Jeanne, and Kevin, loved her much. And the sparkle in her eyes when she was around Victor, and the sparkle in his, told the rest of the story. A match made in heaven; they were perfect together. Both fun loving, hardworking, mischievous, outgoing, genuine—and oh so madly in love!

Crystal, we will always miss your beauty and smile, and especially the beauty that emanated from your heart. A little bit of that heart will remain in ours forever.

Victor, we will be with you soon to begin helping with the physical healing, and to support you through the trying emotional times that lie ahead. Your support group goes far and wide through family and friends; we are all here for you. My heart is broken for you, my son.

My son Kevin needed to express his thoughts about Crystal, too:

This may be too early to write. Maybe I shouldn't write anything at all. But you know what? I'm a writer. I express feelings through fiction, reviews, and the occasional blog post. It helps me think. I don't know if I'm going to do anyone any justice here, but I'm going to at least get some feelings out there. By now there's a good chance that you've heard my sister-in-law, Crystal Rodriguez, died in a tragic accident yesterday. Words cannot describe how this makes me feel, partly because I'm not sure what to feel myself. Angry? Angry at what? It was a parasailing malfunction. Nobody's fault, it's just something that happened one day.

Do I question God and His plan? Maybe, but I do that all the time anyway, so why make this day special? Sad? Yeah . . . that seems like a good place to start. It's the one emotion I can confidently say I know I'm feeling. I guess I'm also a little in denial. Who wouldn't be? I'm scared, I guess. Scared for my brother (her husband), her family, her brothers, and sisters. Part of me wishes that I'd never met her. I hate saying goodbye, and this is about as goodbye as it gets.

No, I'm not insensitive; it's just a defense mechanism. I hate meeting people who I come to genuinely care about only to lose them. I know I'm not the one who's lost the most in all this . . . but boy, it feels like I did. Of course, that's selfish because everyone who knew Crystal has lost something. They've either lost a best friend, a wife, a sister, or simply someone who you gave a couple extra bucks to at Tahoe Joe's because her smile was just SOOOO irresistible! It's hard to be many different kinds of good to many different kinds of people, but somehow, she pulled it off. What's more amazing is that she made it look so easy.

What's more, she managed to get this to spill over into other people and somehow make THEM better people sometimes! Worked with my brother; even worked with me to some extent. She helped me look at the positive side of life more than a few times (something that is not easy to do). So, what do I do now that she's not here to help me think of the positives in life . . . well, just take what I learned from her, I guess? I think back to that Garth Brooks song "The Dance," where he has a night of fun before tragedy strikes in the worst possible way. The message of the song is not defeat though: it's victory. Yeah, he lost someone, but if he had avoided the pain he would have missed out on the dance.

I sort of feel this way now. What's happened hurts. Honestly, as tears come and go as I write this, it just seems to hurt more.

But there is a reason it hurts, I loved Crystal. She was fun, nice, caring, and even funny. I was looking forward to having her in the family. And honestly, even though she was taken from us so early I'm glad she was there in the first place. She made our family better, more complete. The pain we're feeling proves that. I'm going to have those memories for a lifetime, and they will always be there to cheer me up when I need them to. For now, I'm sad and I will likely be sad for a while. But I'm also happy that I got to know her and that she was a big part of my family's life.

Her being so good to everyone was who she was, who she wanted to be. And we're all the more blessed that it was. Again, I don't know if any of this is coming together good. I'm not even sure if it makes sense. But the underlying theme of this is that I feel blessed to have known her and I won't ever forget her. I know she might not be here anymore, but the effect she's had on my entire family will be around for years to come. I don't know what God's plan is, but I thank him for that gift. ". . . Be thou faithful unto death and I will give thee a crown of life."[6]

The next day, our friend Mike drove us to San Francisco so Rubén could get an emergency passport. Since Kevin got in early that morning, he was able to take the drive with us. We received quick assistance at the passport office and by 1:30 PM, Rubén had his passport.

I talked to Victor on the phone before leaving and he said, "Mom, I can't stop crying." I told him that it was okay and that we hadn't stopped crying either. Between tears, I said, "Victor, Crystal changed our lives and now she has changed our lives again."

Our plane was scheduled to leave for Miami at 8:35 PM. We had seven hours in San Francisco before we could leave. We decided to just sit at our terminal. At times we talked or cried and other times we were deep in our own thoughts. Seven hours went by quickly. Actually, we almost missed our flight. We lost track of time until a flurry of texts started coming in saying things like, "You're probably boarding the plane, but I wanted you to know I'm praying." I looked around and noticed that no one was near our gate. I glanced at my watch and realized they were right; we should be boarding yet no one was around. I saw a lady at a counter and told Rubén to ask her what was going on. He didn't move fast enough for me, so I quickly ran over and asked her myself. Come to find out, our gate was changed, and we were at the wrong one. We ran to our terminal and sure enough, everyone had boarded. We were the last ones to arrive!

We got into Miami right around 5:00 AM and had another five hours to wait for our next plane. Since we were there so early, we were again the only ones at the terminal. We continued to grieve the loss of our Crystal and the need to be with our son. Time must have escaped us again because over the intercom, we suddenly heard, "Rodriguez, please check in at the counter." Rubén quickly checked it out and came running back saying, "The plane is ready to leave!" We almost missed our second plane. God was truly looking over us in our fog of grief, pain, and loss.

Chapter Four

THE ARRIVAL
And Attempted Departure

Catastrophic loss wreaks destruction like a massive flood. It is unrelenting, unforgiving, and uncontrollable, brutally erosive to body, mind, and spirit . . . A catastrophic loss leaves the landscape of one's life forever changed.

—Jerry Sittser[7]

WHEN WE LANDED IN the Bahamas, we were greeted by Debbie with the Ministry of Tourism, who whisked us through customs. She then drove us directly to the hospital to see Victor. As we entered the ICU, along with multiple abrasions on the right side of Victor's body, we saw what seemed like tubes and IVs everywhere. Once again, tears welled up in my eyes as I rushed over to kiss his face and hold his hand. We were so happy to see him and yet so heartbroken at the same time.

The first thing Victor said to us was, "The doctor said it's a miracle that I lived, and the nurses said that God has a plan for me." Then, with tears rolling down both of his cheeks he said, "But my plans were with Crystal by my side. What am I to do? What am I to do without Crystal?" And we just wept together. We wept for him, and we wept for ourselves. And I thought to myself, "What *are* we going to do without her?"

Later, we spoke to Victor's doctor, Dr. Ferguson, and that's when we found out that they didn't expect him to live through the first thirty-six hours. He didn't tell us that over the phone because he knew we were already grieving the death of Crystal. He also knew we couldn't get there any faster, so he didn't want us to worry any more than we had to. He, too, told us that it was a miracle that Victor lived.

As we talked to Victor, I expressed my regret that it took so long for us to get to him and that he was all alone. He immediately said, "Mom, I actually wasn't alone. All throughout the night people would come in, lay their hands on me and pray." Tears filled my eyes as I thanked the Lord for answering my prayer that he wouldn't feel so alone.

We asked Victor about the accident, and he told us that he just remembers falling from the parasail and then waking up in the hospital. He asked me if I thought Crystal suffered and I told him I felt Crystal had the same experience as him, that she remembered falling, but instead of waking up in the hospital and seeing the doctors, she opened her eyes and she was in heaven, face to face with Jesus.

That was my only comfort—knowing that she was with the Lord. My heart was aching so badly. Not only for the loss of my sweet Crystal (as if that's not enough pain!) but to hear the anguish in Victor's voice and see it in his face as he dealt with the loss of his wife, his best friend, and his soulmate . . . It was just too much. With tears in his eyes he again asked, "What am I to do? What am I to do without Crystal? I made plans and it was with Crystal by my side." To see him suffer, not only emotionally but physically, was one of the hardest things I've experienced as a mother. He just kept saying, "Why her and not me?" His heart was broken. He had never felt such pain and yet he knew it was a miracle that he lived. Victor knew God had something for him to do because he didn't die but he didn't know what it was. I told him, "For right now, what you need to do, is get better." That's all I could tell him.

That first day we were there, I held Victor's hand all day long. At one point, I could see him fighting to stay awake and I told him he should rest. He looked at me and said, "Will you be here when I wake up?" I told him that I wasn't going anywhere! His reply almost broke me, "Will you stay and hold my hand?" Through tears, I replied, "Of course, I will."

As I sat holding Victor's hand while he finally got some sleep, I looked around the room. This was not the type of hospital room I was used to in the States. The ICU had only four beds. In the corner of the room, there was fly paper hanging from the ceiling, flies attached and all. I looked down at his bed, where there was more rust than not. That's when I noticed that his chest tube simply flowed into a big glass jug. Even with all of that, I was thankful that they saved my son.

Rubén's brother, Manny, flew in Saturday evening and we were so grateful to see him. The next day was Sunday, June 19. It was Father's Day. I was awakened by my phone alarm. As I opened my eyes, Rubén turned off the alarm and promptly started to cry. The background picture on my phone was a photo with the whole family, including Crystal. I got up and we just held each other and wept. I don't know how long we stood there, but we had a good long cry. What a great loss, not only to Victor and to us, but to the world. This one I will never understand . . . I know God has a plan for all of us but what kind of plan is this? So many people are hurting because of Crystal's death. My heart is more than broken, it is shattered into tiny pieces, and I know it'll never be put back the same. We had plans . . . Victor had plans . . . And they all included Crystal.

I talked to God that morning as we got ready for the day. I told Him, "I know your thoughts are not my thoughts and my ways are not your ways. But help me to understand, to grasp or even have a little glimpse of what you were thinking when you allowed this? What could have been your plan when you allowed Crystal to die? I grieve for Crystal and our loss; she touched our lives so much and filled a spot in our heart that was just waiting for her. And yet I am so blessed that Victor lived . . . the doctors say it's a miracle that he survived, and I thank You for his life! I can't even comprehend how it would have been if I had lost them both. I have such great sorrow deep in my heart over Crystal's death, but I know if Victor died too, it would have been sorrow upon sorrow. But even as I grieve, there is a peace in knowing that Crystal is with You. But this is all just so hard."

As we entered Victor's room, he smiled softly and said, "Happy Father's Day! But, Dad, I don't have a gift for you." Rubén teared up and said, "You are my gift—you are alive!" Then Victor's face lit up as he remembered that Crystal bought a Father's Day gift for Rubén. He told his dad that as they were going through the marketplace, Crystal saw a little bottle of Puerto Rican rum and said, "And this is for Pops for Father's Day!"

One of the things Victor told us on the day we arrived was that the hospital had wanted him to identify Crystal's body. Apparently, this was both a hospital and a morgue. I couldn't believe that they actually planned to wheel Victor, in his hospital bed (because he was in such critical condition that he couldn't be put in a wheelchair) to the morgue to identify her body. He told them he couldn't do it and that they needed to wait until we arrived.

So, there we were, Rubén, his brother Manny, and me walking down through the hospital to the morgue. Manny took a seat against the wall as the doctor brought Rubén and me over to the glass window. He then pulled the curtain so we could identify her body.

To see her body there before us . . . not living . . . To see her cute little button nose and her beautifully shaped eyebrows . . . It just made it real. We stood there, holding each other with a never-ending flow of tears running down our cheeks. We nodded to the doctor, "Yes, that is Crystal." It was so agonizing . . . So excruciating . . . Almost unbearable! How could they have expected Victor to identify her?

As we got back to Victor's room, we talked about Crystal—who she was to us and all about her life. Victor told us how they were going to get a turtle when they got back home. They had a name and everything—Herbert. He also said, "Mom, I just keep expecting her to come through the door." Then, with so much pain in his voice, he said, "I don't even know what day it is . . . my days stopped when Crystal died."

We spent most of the day remembering, crying, and talking about our beautiful Crystal. Oh, how my heart aches as I see my son suffer so much. And to see my husband cry as he talks about "Cutes." That's the nickname he gave her so many years ago . . . It's unbearable! She truly was our daughter and we loved her, and she *knew* we loved her. She made us better as a family.

We spent our days at the hospital. We arrived every day at 9:00 AM and left at 8:00 PM. They made us leave for a few hours at lunch time and then kicked us out every night. If I had it my way, we would have been there twenty-four hours a day!

It was Tuesday the 21st, six days after the accident and I woke up at 5:15 AM. I just couldn't sleep . . . I woke up sad, so incredibly sad. I was still grappling with her death. We loved her so, so much. Victor loved her so incredibly much. We made her happy and she made us happy. She loved everyone, and they couldn't help but love her back.

Even though I was emotionally exhausted, I couldn't seem to sleep more than five hours at night and even then, I tossed and turned. I laid in bed, everyone else still asleep, and I yearned to hear Crystal's voice. So, I grabbed my phone and looked through my voicemails. That's when I realized that I only had one voicemail from Crystal. We always communicated so much via text. And the times when she did call, I always tried to pick up. Now I regretted that I didn't have more voicemails with her sweet, loving voice.

As I looked at my phone, I saw that I had a text from my friend Joanna. She wrote, "I do believe God's heart is broken for you and that He alone will be the one to hold you together. But I wish I could say something that would somehow give you what you need to be able to understand." Messages like these from my friends helped me during the coming weeks and months.

Like every day, we got ready and went to see Victor. As we arrived, he started tearing up. "I cry just thinking about her name, Mom and Dad." I told him that he must remember how happy she was—she had a husband who loved her and whom she loved. We became her parents, we loved and adored her, and she loved us just as much. Together, they enjoyed a beautiful wedding where everyone danced the night away. And they had an exciting honeymoon doing everything Crystal enjoyed. I said, "Victor, she got everything she wanted." He started crying and interrupted me, "She wanted to be a mom and I wanted to be a father." He paused and then continued, "We even picked names. If it was a boy, his name would be Noah Anthony Rodriguez after Dad (Rubén's middle name is Anthony) and if it was a girl . . . Brenna." We sat there and cried together as we thought about what could have been.

I started thinking about the many times that we dreamed together over the years. Crystal always went on family trips and vacations with us even before they were married. So, it didn't seem unusual to talk to them about future vacations and plans. One night, we had taken them out to our favorite Mexican restaurant. We talked about going on vacation together when they had children . . . about getting two condos with our timeshares so that we could watch the grandkids at night, and they could have time together.

Crystal would have been a beautiful and wonderful mom and Victor would have been a great dad. They both loved children, and kids loved them! It was so hard to think of what would have been . . . of what could have been. We always said how Kevin would make such a great uncle . . . How he would take his nieces and nephews to all the movies and get them into Disneyland . . .

Victor still wasn't doing well. In addition to the emotional turmoil he was in, he physically hurt everywhere, too. He couldn't move much without excruciating pain throughout his whole body. Plus, he didn't have much of an appetite. Everything seemed to make him queasy. He developed internal bleeding and the doctor had to give him two units of blood because his hemoglobin dropped to close to half of what it should have been. Dr. Theo explained that with blunt force trauma, sometimes problems don't show up until days later. He compared it to a bruise—when you get hit in the eye, you don't see the bruise until days later. The same was true of Victor's injuries.

They performed a CT scan on Victor's liver and spleen but didn't need to do one on the kidneys since there was no blood in his urine. After undergoing the CT, they determined the cause . . . Both Victor's liver and spleen were damaged by the trauma of the fall. There was fluid around not only the liver and spleen but also the pelvis. The good news was that both were intact, so Victor didn't need to have surgery. There was evidence of a contusion in the liver, but the doctor wanted to take a conservative approach. He wanted to watch it closely to see if Victor would need more blood. Dr. Theo wanted Victor to rest and allow God to do His work in healing him.

Even though Victor had a wonderful nursing staff, and his doctor was not only informative but also extremely caring with a wonderful bedside manner, I wanted Victor to be flown to a hospital in the United States. I wasn't comfortable with the fact that he needed blood and they didn't have an MRI machine at the hospital. Both Rubén and I expressed to Dr. Theo that we wanted Victor moved and he said he would check into that for us.

Finally, six days after the accident, Victor was off oxygen! As you can imagine, he was anxious to get off the island. We all were ... But there were so many things to coordinate. We decided to have Victor medevacked to Florida instead of California because of the cost. We were quoted $75,000 to fly to California and only $10,800 to Florida. Not that we had $10,800 lying around, but we did have a credit card that could at least handle that amount. Plus, Rubén's oldest brother Eddie and his wife Maria lived in Orlando. They graciously offered for us to stay with them while Victor was in the hospital.

We were in a holding pattern while we waited to hear if the doctor was able to find a hospital for Victor. We knew it wasn't going to be as easy as it sounded. After all, the hospital had to have a trauma unit and a doctor who would oversee Victor's care. In addition to that, we would need the hospital and that doctor to accept Victor, with no insurance.

Later that Wednesday afternoon, the nurse told me I had a call from Orlando Regional Medical Center. As I picked up, a woman introduced herself as Yvonne and told me she was the hospital coordinator. She said she heard we wanted to medevac our son to their hospital. I told her that was correct, and she said she had a few questions. I was able to answer all her questions until she said, "Who is he insured by and what is his policy number?" I said, "Didn't the doctor tell you? Victor has no insurance." There was a long pause; it was almost deafening. She finally said something, "Ohhhh, well . . . since this is an international case, we will have to send it to the board to review. That will take 2–3 days before we'll know the outcome."

As I listened, I just knew it wouldn't be approved. That's when I heard myself say, "Yvonne, do you know his story?" She said yes and quickly began stating facts, "He has six broken ribs, a punctured lung, a lacerated liver and spleen . . ." I stopped her and said, "No, do you know his *story*? Do you know that he just got married and was on his honeymoon? Do you know that the day before they were to come home, they went parasailing? Do you know that there was an equipment malfunction and that they fell over eighty feet? Do you know that his wife died? Do you know that this is a young man who wants and needs to come back to the States? Do you know *this* story?" Yvonne took a deep breath and replied, "No, I didn't know that story." I could hear tears in her voice as she continued, "I'll do everything that I can."

I sent word to all my family and friends to pray that they would approve the transfer. I understood that the likelihood of it happening was slim because Victor had no insurance and, at that point, the doctors in the Bahamas felt he wasn't considered critical any longer. The danger point had passed and technically the hospital here in the Bahamas could take care of him.

It was in the afternoon when the nurse told me that I had another call from Orlando Regional Hospital. I was surprised because only a day had passed since my conversation with Yvonne. She told me that she had wonderful news, "Jeanne, the trauma unit approved the transfer and there is a bed waiting whenever you're ready to travel." The best part was when she told me the name of the doctor overseeing Victor's case. She first spelled it, P-R-O-M-E-S and then pronounced it . . . Dr. Promise! At that moment, one of *God's* promises popped into my mind. That promise is, "I will never leave nor forsake you."[8]

About the same time, I received a text from another friend, Julie. Her text said she read something in her devotional that morning and wanted to pass it along, "My continual Presence is a promise, guaranteeing that you never have to face anything alone."[9] She thought it was amazing that today we found out Victor's doctor's name was Dr. Promes (Promise).

But before we could leave the Bahamas and head to Florida, the hard part came . . . I had to finish packing up Crystal's belongings. At first, Rubén questioned why we were bringing anything back. But how could we not?—it would be like leaving a part of her behind. That night, as I put each piece of her clothing in the suitcase, I remembered her. It is hard to express exactly how I felt as I folded her clothes, but I felt honored to do what a mom would do when her child dies. I always felt she was the daughter I never had. Rubén and I both felt that way and we were blessed to have her in our family. She had truly become the heart of our family. And as a friend said, "Only God can fill the hole she leaves."

Crystal and I were so much alike. And as I put her books in the suitcase, I was reminded of that . . . how we both loved to read . . . and of her love of Francine Rivers. And then other memories began to flow. Her new dresses made me think about the day she called me to tell me what she'd gotten. She wanted me to come over right away so she could show them to me . . . There was a cute white dress for the dress rehearsal and two others perfect for the Bahamas. She tried each one on and twirled around asking me what I thought. She beamed! I smiled as I recalled her delight. I came across a bottle of her fragrance and decided to put that in my purse. It took me hours to finish packing her suitcase; memories kept flooding in as I placed each of her belongings into the luggage, knowing she would never use them again.

The last thing we had to do was pick up Crystal's ashes. It seemed like just yesterday that Victor and Crystal got their engagement pictures taken and now this . . . Speaking of photos, they loved having those photos taken and my friend Tori did such a wonderful job! Victor and Crystal loved Tori. They had such fun with her, and I know she loved spending time with them, too! They had looked forward to going to San Francisco to get additional wedding pictures when they got back from their honeymoon, but obviously those would never happen now.

I'm so glad that Tori was able to photograph the happiest moments in their lives. She was able to capture their personalities on film and we'll always have them to remember how they loved each other, and that is a gift. Those photos are bittersweet though. As much as my heart is filled with joy in seeing their love for each other, it also breaks every time as I'm reminded that their life together ended far too quickly.

Chapter Five

BACK TO THE STATES
And a Media Blitz

The place where you continually return for love and acceptance—that's home.
—Richelle E. Goodrich[10]

THE NEXT MIRACLE IS the flight. Originally, Air Ambulance Services quoted us a price of $10,800 to fly from the Bahamas (Freeport) to Orlando, Florida. But since Victor's health had improved enough that he wouldn't need a doctor on board (just a nurse) the cost went down to $9,600.

The morning we were to pay for the medevac, I remembered something my friend said to me when she came by the house on the day of the accident. Cathy Yanez told me that Bayside Church was receiving calls from people who heard what happened and they wanted to donate money to help us with expenses. She then told me that a memorial fund was started for our family.

So, that morning, I called her and told her that we were having Victor medevacked to Florida. She asked me the cost. When I told her what we needed, she assured me that enough money came in to cover the cost. Rubén and I were absolutely overwhelmed by the generosity of our church family. I could see the Lord's hand in it all!

So, on Friday, June 24, nine days after the accident, Manny flew home to his family in New York and Rubén, and I flew to Florida with

Victor. I carried Crystal's remains in a little box on my lap as we took the next step in Victor's healing journey. Originally, I was going to be the only one to fly with Victor since the plane could only hold five, but now that Victor only needed a nurse, that left a spot for Rubén! I was so thankful that we could all travel together.

As we waited for the plane to take off, we could hear loud booms of thunder, accompanying the torrential downpour of rain. As I looked out my window, I had a quiet conversation with God. "Lord, help me in my brokenness. I haven't lost my faith, but I just don't understand." I watched the rain fall and wept as my heart broke even more over the loss of our precious Crystal. To me, the rain was a representation of all the tears that have been shed over her death. That day, we picked up her ashes and it was a reminder, once again, that she was gone from us, and it wouldn't be until our lives were over before we'd see her again. As we left Freeport, Victor turned to me and said, "I've never felt so loved and so alone at the same time." And I, too, felt that same sentiment.

We arrived at Orlando Regional Medical Hospital and were warmly greeted by Carol, the nurse in charge for the evening. She wrapped her arm around my shoulder and pulled me close as she said, "We're going to take good care of your son." And with that, I burst into tears. It was so good to be back in the United States with all the latest equipment! They put us in a big, beautiful private room in the ICU. It was so vastly different than his room in the Bahamas that Victor said, "This is like being at the Ritz!" The room also had a Murphy's bed so one of us could always be with him. The first couple of days and nights, I didn't leave his side.

Since there was only a single size bed in Victor's room, we would still need a place for one of us to stay. We were blessed that Rubén's brother and his wife (Eddie and Maria) took us in. Every night one of us stayed in their home. When they said "Yes" to us staying there, they had no idea we'd be there for over a month. Let's be honest, neither did we.

It seemed like every day someone sent an encouraging word. The day after we arrived in Orlando, a stranger sent this message to me,

"We are never promised that everything in life will be as we hope and dream. In fact, those who have faith in God understand that we will suffer in this life. Yet, we believe that in God's sovereignty, He is ultimately in control of all things. Whether He chooses to allow suffering, or to spare us from suffering, has to do with a wisdom that is His alone and which we do not possess. A parent loves a child and has compassion when they suffer. So, God loves us compassionately and grieves over what happened to Victor and Crystal. He will be with Victor in every moment of his suffering and healing. He will carry Victor through and comfort him as no one else can. We must look beyond this present life and have faith that we all will be well in eternity. All wrongs will be made right, and every tear will be wiped from our eyes. As we pray to God and pour out our hearts to Him, we need to trust Him to answer according to His wisdom. None of this will make sense unless we first trust in His love for us. As we grow closer to God, His love for us overcomes our weakness, doubt and fear."[11]

It had been ten days since I found out our beloved Crystal died. I woke up again, with tears in my eyes as I remembered that Crystal really wasn't with us. I couldn't stop the tears . . . As I got dressed, I noticed her fragrance bottle on the dresser, and I decided to wear it to feel close to her. About the same time, my friend Joanna texted me something from her devotional. "You have journeyed up a steep rugged path in recent days. The way ahead is shrouded in uncertainty. Look neither behind you nor before you. Instead, focus your attention on Me, your constant companion. Trust that I will equip you fully for whatever awaits you on your journey. I designed time to be a protection for you. You couldn't bear to see all your life at once. Though I am unlimited by time, it is the present moment that I meet you. Refresh yourself in My company, breathing deep draughts of My Presence. The highest level of trust is to enjoy Me, moment by moment. I am with you, watching over you wherever you go."[12]

As we stayed by Victor's side, we learned that several news organizations were calling my work to find out more information. One of Victor's friends had gotten a message through Facebook from *ABC*

News wanting to ask her questions about Victor and Crystal. We got a call from *New York Daily News* expressing an interest in doing an interview and we received word that *Good Morning America* wanted to fly us to New York for an interview as well. We turned them all down. We didn't want to take any time away from the care of our son, but we did give permission to some of Victor and Crystal's friends to speak to local news and *The Sacramento Bee*.

Chapter Six

ANOTHER MIRACLE
And a Setback

Out of difficulties grow miracles.
—Jean de la Bruyere

WHEN VICTOR WAS MEDEVACKED to the hospital in Florida, they immediately started running tests. All throughout that first night, they came into his room and whisked him off for various tests . . . a CT scan, an MRI, and various others. They concluded that he needed a stent in one of the bile ducts to stop the leakage. So that afternoon, 10 days after the accident, Victor was into surgery, and we waited for the results.

As I was waiting, my phone rang. Since the accident, I rarely picked up the phone. I generally let it go straight to voicemail but this time, I looked to see who was calling. It was Nancy from work. I was about to turn my phone off when I felt a prompting to answer it.

Nancy said a quick hello and started straight into what felt like a lengthy monologue. She was telling me about a leaders' meeting she was hosting at her house. "Jeanne, I was about to go to the store to get some pastries," she said. I couldn't believe my ears . . . pastries? She called to tell me about pastries!? She continued, "I was planning to go to a local spot but felt the Lord wanted me to go to another store. It's a bit further, but has better pastries, so I figured God wanted to bless the leaders." By now, I was about to scream. In fact, in my mind, I was screaming already, "Are you kidding me?!" Right about then, she said, "Jeanne, I quickly discovered why I was really at that pastry shop. I ran into Leanne, an old friend whom I hadn't seen in about ten years. We caught up a bit and then she started to talk about Victor and Crystal. She asked if I knew the family and of course I told her that we work together. I don't know why or how it came up, but I mentioned that Victor would eventually need to be medevacked back to California. That's when she mentioned another friend who lives in Orlando. That friend has a medevac business." Nancy then went on to give me his name and number. After getting over my initial frustration, I was very happy that I answered the phone and couldn't wait to see how the Lord might use this connection.

Rubén and I had already started to check out what it would cost to get Victor home and the prices varied from $45,000–$65,000. At those prices, medevacking wasn't an option, but neither was staying in Orlando long term. I called Nancy's friend of a friend about the medevac, and he already knew our situation. "When Victor is stable enough, I will medevac him to Sacramento for $25,000," he went on to say. My heart dropped. $25,000! Sure, that's better than $45,000 or $65,000 but where were we going to get that kind of money? I thanked him and hung up. I immediately started talking to God. "What was that all about? Sure, it's a lot less than anyone else quoted, but who has that kind of money?" I was disappointed and confused. Honestly, I thought God was going to do another miracle and provide transportation again.

A few hours later, I get a call from Mark. He was a volunteer from church that was handling all the media inquiries that were coming in. It seemed that our local paper, *The Sacramento Bee*, did a story about Victor and Crystal's accident and it was on the front page. He had received a call from the Automobile Association of Greater Sacramento (AAGS), and they didn't just want to donate money, they wanted to do something specific to meet a need that Victor had. I told Mark that the only thing he needed was a medevac to bring him home when he was stable enough.

Mark told me to get some prices and call him back. Before he could hang up, I said, "Mark, I actually have a price. It's $25,000." "Thanks," he replied. "Do you need anything else?" He asked because he didn't expect the AAGS to put out that kind of money. "Honestly, Mark," I continued, "there really isn't anything else that we need." I thanked him for handling all these details for us. He said that it would probably be a while before he'd get back to me as AAGS would need time to discuss such a large donation.

Less than an hour later, the phone rang. It was Mark again. I figured he had another question or inquiry but apparently the Automobile Association of Greater Sacramento decided to pick up the full cost of the medevac to Sacramento! Wow! Wow! Wow!

But amid such a tremendous celebration, we ran into another setback. We had hoped that the doctors could put a stent in one of the bile ducts to stop the leakage. They couldn't find the duct so instead, they had to take the drain out of the abdomen and place one near the liver instead.

Dr. Feuer came in that night reporting that he wasn't happy with the amount of bile flowing out. He had consulted with another surgeon in Gainesville who specializes in endoscopic retrograde cholangiopancreatography (ERCP). That's where the surgeon goes down the throat to get to the bile duct. He said if the laceration didn't heal on its own (there's a ten to fifty percent chance it will), they would move Victor to another hospital in Florida for the procedure to be done. Before he could continue, I asked, "Do you think that UC Davis in California would have a specialist?" He was fairly certain that they did. "But how would you get Victor there?" he asked. That's when I told him all about the local dealership who offered to pay the cost of the medevac. He looked surprised and said, "Do you know how much that is going to cost?" When I answered, "Yes, $25,000!" He couldn't believe that someone would do that for Victor and our family!

Once again, we put a request out to our family, friends, and church and asked for prayer for Victor. Now that we had a plan to get Victor home, we were anxious to make it happen!

The next morning, five doctors showed up. They were cautiously optimistic that the duct would heal on its own. Apparently, the bilirubin count was down from the day before and they felt that if the count continued to decrease, the laceration would heal on its own. If everything went well, Victor would be discharged on Saturday. He would have to keep the drain in for another three or four days before he'd return to have that removed. And then Victor would still have to rest up for a few days before he'd be cleared to travel. But they hoped he would be flying home on Monday, July 11. We were overjoyed and so we started praying that we would, in fact, return home on July 11!

Chapter Seven

SURPRISES

And So Much Generosity

*I always love to be careful with my expectations so that life
has pleasant surprises for me.*

—Sebastian Thrun[13]

DURING HIS TIME IN the hospital, family and friends tried to think
of ways to keep Victor's spirits lifted. He's a die-hard Oakland A's fan,
so when he received a call from A's pitcher, Dallas Braden, he was so
pumped. He couldn't believe he actually had a conversation with *the*
Dallas Braden. Go A's!

Victor's brother Kevin pulled off another huge surprise. One
night the phone rang, and Rubén answered. "It's Ryan Reynolds . . .
the actor . . . for you," he said as he passed the phone to Victor. Victor
smirked thinking it was a joke, but it wasn't! He could hardly believe it,
"Are you kidding me?" he replied. Ryan is hands down Victor's favorite
actor and somehow Kevin had gotten ahold of Ryan's PR person, and
they arranged the call. As Victor grabbed the phone, he said, "My
man!" He then launched into a conversation led by how big of a fan
he's been for the past seven years. They talked quite a bit, including
Victor's injuries and his plans on moving back in with us.

Ryan then went on to invite Victor down to the premiere of
his new movie *The Change-Up*. The plan was that Ryan would fly
Victor and a guest down to the Hollywood premiere. Ryan would

then personally meet both of them. The call and the anticipation of this once-in-a-lifetime experience lifted Victor's spirits so much. Even though the premiere was over a month away, Victor unfortunately was not able to attend because he wasn't fully healed by then.

There were so many sweet surprises that came over the coming weeks and months. Whether it was a care package with A's gear or Victor's favorite candy bars or some movies to help pass the time, each surprise was sweet. We were constantly reminded that we were surrounded by a community who genuinely loved and cared for us.

Around the same time these surprises were pouring in, we found out that Victor's friends were raising money to help with the expenses. They were hosting a fundraiser at a local spot, Cool Hand Luke's, and all the tips from that one evening were going into the care fund that our church had created for Victor. His friend Jim Coomes sent over some pictures from the event, but Victor only made it through the first photo. It was a picture of his friends Chris and Dolly. Dolly was wearing a shirt with a big heart on it, and it read "Rodriguez" along the top. She was also wearing a pin with a picture of Crystal on it. Victor started crying uncontrollably as soon as he saw the shirt and the pin. Then, of course, we all began to cry. We couldn't look at any photos after that. But we did get an update from Jim that a businessman had come into Luke's and upon hearing about the fundraiser, said he would match the amount raised. The generosity of people, those we know and those we don't, has touched my heart like never before.

Chapter Eight

BEING RELEASED

Or So We Hoped

*So do not fear, for I am with you; do not be dismayed, for
I am your God. I will strengthen you and help you; I will
uphold you with my righteous right hand.*

—Isaiah 41:10[14]

VICTOR WAS TEMPORARILY RELEASED on Friday, July 1, and was scheduled to come back to the hospital on Tuesday for the removal of the drain. The doctors believed that we could do at home what they were doing in the hospital and that getting out of the hospital would be good for Victor's spirits. We completely agreed! Our only focus was monitoring his bile outtake and getting some food into him. Since the accident, Victor had lost twenty pounds and he was looking so very thin.

Victor *loves* Chinese food, so that was a no-brainer for dinner upon his release! But in the end, Victor only ate two small pieces of General's chicken and three bites of fried rice. He was too full to even eat a single bite of shrimp and he absolutely *loves* shrimp.

My sister Mary flew down from New Jersey to comfort us and provide some much-needed moral support. She encouraged us in so many ways. One story she shared, just hit home. At her last Book Club, they prayed for Victor, our family, and Crystal's family. That might not seem like much, but what's incredible is that this group has been together for over eight years. They have a mixture of faiths and religions and over the course of those eight years, they'd never prayed together before. Victor and Crystal and their tragedy were bringing people together in such deep ways.

It was just so nice to have Victor and my sister all together with Eddie, Maria, Rubén, and myself. I felt like I could breathe for the first time in sixteen days. In fact, that night was the first night that I was in bed by 9:30 PM. Since we had gotten the news of the accident, I hadn't climbed into bed any night before midnight. And most nights, it was closer to 1:00 or 2:00 AM. I was so hopeful that we would soon be bringing Victor home that I slept so soundly that night.

As each day passed, Victor seemed to get weaker and weaker. By the time Tuesday arrived, he had begun throwing up and was starting to run a fever. Following check in, we learned that we had to get more lab work done and, once again, they had trouble drawing his blood. Once the labs were complete, we headed to our appointment. We could see the look of concern on the faces of the medical staff as they walked into Victor's room. His white count was at thirty-three. I had no point of reference, and so I asked what it should be. A nurse replied, "It should be around eleven. Thirty-three indicates that there's an infection."

And so, Victor was readmitted to the hospital. While they were trying to find a bed in the trauma unit, they placed him in a hold room. That's where they took his 103 temperature. Victor was so dehydrated on top of everything else that they had to put the saline on "push" so they could get it into his system quickly. As if that weren't enough, there was more blood work to be done, too! I told his nurse, Mary, how much trouble people were having drawing his blood. She called in their best . . . a nurse named Janice. Janice not only had success on drawing the blood, but she came through on the first time! She went two for two without any problems. For that, Victor told her that he loved her.

After the blood draw, they did another CT scan and found that there were four pockets of bile. And so, Victor was scheduled for surgery the following morning.

Right after we finished up all the scans and tests and blood draws, they were finally able to find a bed in the trauma unit and they wheeled Victor up. Upon our arrival, we were happy to see a familiar face . . . It was his nurse Chris, the same nurse Victor had when we first arrived from the Bahamas. That night Rubén stayed with Victor, and I stayed at his brother's house.

Chapter Nine

THE FOG

A Birthday to Remember

*In tragedy, it's hard to find a good resolution; it's not black
and white: it's a big fog of gray.*

—Paul Dano

SO MANY MORNINGS THERE would be a moment between sleeping and waking when everything was good. My mind would temporarily forget about the accident. It was a split second of peace. Then, my mind and body would fully awaken, and I wouldn't know where I was. I didn't recognize anything in the room. As I'd look around, I'd finally realize that I was in my brother-in-law's house. That's when it would hit me again . . . Victor was in the hospital. Crystal was dead. And then the deepest of sorrows would wash over me again. It was like a scab being picked off day after day. The wound was deep and every time it was exposed, it hurt all over again. Today was one of those mornings, one of those painful, exposed mornings.

As I lay there feeling immense sorrow, I began to wonder how many mornings this very thing happened to Victor. Sadness doesn't even begin to describe the emotion. Grief . . . Anguish . . . Loss . . . Tragedy . . . These are not sentiments he should be experiencing so soon after his wedding, yet these feelings made regular daily appearances.

Two days later, it was my birthday. I was about to turn fifty-six and there I was sitting in a hospital with my twenty-two-year-old son

59

who had lost his wife just twenty-four days earlier. I will never understand God's plan in this. And if I'm honest, knowing why will never change the hurt I'm experiencing, or anyone else's for that matter.

But somehow, amidst all the agony, I was able to recognize the blessings. The blessing that my son was alive . . . that he was in one of the best trauma hospitals in the United States . . . that we have family to stay with in Orlando . . . that my sister came down to be with us . . . that we have such good and faithful friends . . . It was still so very hard, but I was thankful for God's goodness in the middle of such pain.

My sister left on July 7th, and Victor's good friend Josh Roome flew in from California the next day to visit him. The 9th was my birthday, so since Josh was with Victor, Rubén and I decided to go to the movies and out to dinner. As we sat at the Olive Garden Restaurant, Rubén and I reminisced about how the first time we met Crystal we were at an Olive Garden. We talked about that first meeting and so many other memories of Crystal and Victor. We laughed and smiled and shed a lot of tears.

After dinner, we headed back to Eddie and Maria's, and there waiting for me were two boxes of flowers, a package, and so many cards. The first box was from my Friday morning Bible study, The Beauties. It had two dozen roses with a note, "Beautiful Jeanne: Although you may not feel celebratory, The Beauties wanted to remember your birthday, and this is our way of dumping a truckload of love on you! Happy Birthday, Beautiful! Love, The Beauties." The second box was a gift from my friend Cathy Yanez. It was the "Sunshine Angel," and she was holding a bunch of sunflowers. It was beautiful and especially meaningful because sunflowers were Crystal's favorite. In the other box of flowers were sunflowers from Chris and Dolly, Victor and Crystal's good friends. They were just thinking of me.

Chapter Ten

ANOTHER SETBACK

And the Onset of Depression

You keep track of all my sorrows. You have collected all
my tears in your bottle. You have recorded each one in
your book.

Psalm 56:8[15]

IT SEEMS THAT EVERY time we get two steps ahead, we end up going back one.

It had been twenty-four days since Victor went into the hospital and he just took another step backwards. It was already a rough day for Victor . . . He was in pain and having trouble breathing. That meant that the doctor had to put a chest tube back in. It's a painful procedure and I can't stand seeing Victor suffer so much. But as soon as they put it in, a liter of fluid came out and he started breathing a little easier.

The doctors shared with us that they felt the tube had been taken out too early when Victor was in the Bahamas. When they initially ran all the tests, they saw fluid but had hoped it would get better on its own. Since that didn't happen, we now just had to be patient and let his body heal. It was a setback for us and another huge disappointment. This setback meant that we weren't flying home by July 11th. And while we were thankful to be out of the Bahamas, we were ready to be home.

For the remainder of the day, Victor was a bit cranky and a little irritable. I knew it was because he too was discouraged. And scared.

But he gradually began showing improvements. So much so, that he was moved out of the trauma unit and settled in a new room. His breathing had improved since they put in the chest tube and by the time he was settled in his new room, he had become more himself. When his nurse Rose came in, she told him she would be with him until 7:00 AM. With a twinkle in his eyes, he excitedly replied, "Oh good, because I'll be here until then, too."

But as each day passed, Rubén and I could see that depression was kicking in. Victor's irritability was met with immense heaviness. You could see it on his face and hear it in his voice. We were getting worried about him. I mean, we all thought we would have been home by now and here it was, almost four weeks later, and Victor still had a tube in his chest and an IV in his arm.

Among other things, the doctors wanted Victor to get out of bed and sit in the chair they had in his room. But Victor had no interest. It was painful for him to get up and he just wanted to lie in bed. We could see and feel the anguish washing over him. He wanted to be home, especially for the softball tournament fundraiser that his friends had planned. It set in that that wasn't going to happen . . . July 16 and 17 were all too close and Victor was far too far from recovery to travel.

Chapter Eleven

THE SOFTBALL FUNDRAISER

Down & Dirty

Friends show their love in times of trouble, not in happiness.

—Euripides

VICTOR AND CRYSTAL WERE on an indoor softball team together and when their friends learned about the accident, they were overwhelmed with heartache and wanted to do something to help. So, they decided to host a fundraiser at the softball arena where they all played.

Dolly, Sarah, Troy, Chris, Brian, Brandie, Shawn, Jim, Ed, and several other close friends pored over every aspect of the tournament trying to get each detail just right. Their softball family pulled together for one of their own and it was incredible to watch! No one hesitated to jump in or offer help. Their love for Victor and Crystal was genuine and it was apparent.

So, on July 16 and 17, 2011, Arena Softball in Roseville, California, hosted a tournament to benefit Victor and honor Crystal. Hundreds of people attended, and thirty softball teams participated. The community responded so generously with raffle prizes, silent auction items, and volunteering their time. It was astounding to see the support from the community. People who didn't even know the bride and groom attended the fundraiser. It really did lift Victor's spirits to see his friends and so many strangers come together to honor Crystal.

I learned over the years that indoor softball is quite different than outdoor softball. The entire field is covered with a tight net to keep the ball in play. There's no foul territory and the game is fast paced. Each team may have a maximum of nine players. Regular games have three innings, whereas championship games play four innings. They are given twenty pitches each inning. The traditional three outs do not end an inning with indoor softball. There are no foul balls, and all hit balls are live. Fly balls caught off the net result in the batter being out. There is no bunting, stealing, leading off base, take-out slides, or blocking a base.

Teams can score on defense as well as offense. The fielding side gets awarded a half run for every out. Two balls are a walk, and two strikes are an out. The batting side gets awarded a half run for every walk and each batter will start with a count of one ball and one strike. To get a homerun, there is an area that is clearly marked and any ball that hits in that area is an automatic homerun.

The weekend was phenomenal! Since Victor couldn't be there in person, one of his friends set it up so that they were able to Skype across the two days. Victor got to talk to many of his friends and he was even able to watch their softball team, Down & Dirty, play in the tournament.

Down & Dirty ended up playing in the championship game against their archrivals, Ruff Ryders. In previous tournaments, it was almost always Down & Dirty vs. Ruff Ryders in the championship game. This tournament was no different. And when these two teams played, it was always a competitive game! Both on and off the field, these teams didn't really like each other; they were true rivals.

As you can imagine, the game was even more competitive than normal. The whole game, the score was neck and neck, right up until the nail-biting end! Ruff Ryders was in the field and Down & Dirty was up to bat. In indoor softball, it's better to be on the field (defense) last since you can gain more points with outs. Ruff Ryders had the upper hand.

As the pitch count for Down & Dirty started to go down, it looked like they might lose. You could feel the despair as it started to spread throughout the team. This was a tournament for Victor and Crystal, after all, and they felt the pressure to win. One player was so upset, she went down to the end of the dugout, sat on the floor, and just started to cry. Another teammate quickly walked over and sat down beside her.

There were two pitches left in the game. Jim Coomes and Brian Schweppe were the last two up to bat. Down & Dirty was down by four and a half runs with the bases loaded. It seemed like a loss was inevitable. That's when Jim stepped up to bat and hit a grand slam. The crowd went nuts with excitement, but it wasn't over yet; they still were behind. The only way Down & Dirty could win was if they scored another homerun. Brian stepped up to plate and the whole building went silent. The pitcher wound up, pitched the ball, and Brian hit the homerun. He won the game for Crystal, for Victor and for Down & Dirty!

Victor, Rubén, and I watched the whole game in his hospital room, right down to Down & Dirty erupting in a victory cheer, jumping on top of each other and hugging. Emotions were high as they stormed the field in celebration! Then we heard the start of a chant . . . It was slow and quiet and grew louder and louder, "Crystal. Crystal. Crystal . . ." As I listened to the chants, chants of those we knew and loved and chants of complete strangers, tears streamed down my cheeks. They were both tears of joy and tears of sadness.

Back in Florida, Victor's fluid output was decreasing every day and we were hoping by the next day that the doctor would take out his chest tube and possibly the two drains that were near his liver and in his abdomen. If this happened, we hoped that we would be able to go home in a few days.

So, four days later, on July 21, we got the good news that Victor was going to be discharged and we could go home. However, the doctors decided that it was best if the chest tube was kept in until Victor got back to California, but they did remove the drains. Rubén and I joined Victor as he was medevacked back home. We left out of the Executive Airport in Orlando, Florida, and had to stop to refuel in Texas. While the plane was being refueled, I checked my messages. That's when I found out that there would be several reporters waiting for us at the airport. We flew to Sacramento McClellan Airport where an ambulance was waiting to whisk Victor to the Sutter Roseville Medical Center. As Victor was being taken to the ambulance, I talked to the news reporters who were there, ready with questions. This gave me an opportunity to tell them how appreciative we were of all the prayers and generous support that we received from the community.

Chapter Twelve

FIRST SUNDAY BACK

Do You Trust Me?

Those who suffer loss live suspended between a past for which they long and a future for which they hope . . . Memories of the past only remind them of what they have lost; hope for the future only taunts them with an unknown too remote even to imagine.

—Jerry Sittser[16]

IT'S GOOD TO BE home! I can't believe it's been almost six weeks since the accident. That Sunday, I decided to go to church with my friend Joanna. It was the first time I'd been to church since the accident, and I really didn't know what to expect. One of my pastors, Curt Harlow, was teaching about the questions that Jesus asked people:

- "What is it you want?"[17]
- "What do you want me to do for you?"[18]
- "Why are you troubled, and why do doubts rise in your minds?"[19]

Then Curt asked, "What question is Jesus asking you?" He paused. That's when I realized that he wanted us to actually ask God the question. So, as I sat there, I asked the Lord if there was anything He wanted to ask me. If I'm honest, I really wasn't expecting to hear anything. Then the Lord spoke to my heart, "Do you trust me?" I pondered that for a long time, replaying His question over and over in my mind. "Do you trust me?" Honestly, I got so lost in that question that I couldn't tell you anything else Curt said that morning.

Following the service, I turned to Joanna and told her what the Lord asked. I said, "Joanna, if He asked me, 'Do you love me?' I could easily say yes. If He asked me, 'Do you believe in me?' I could easily reply yes. On June 15th, if He asked me, 'Do you trust me?' I could have easily answered yes. But, today, I don't know how to answer that specific question." She simply sat and listened. She reached over and grabbed my hand and just let me ponder over that question for quite some time.

Out of all the questions, why would He ask *that* one? All day long, I just couldn't get it out of my head. Later on, I came to realize that there was a reason God asked that particular question . . . "Do you trust me?" God knows that trust is of the utmost importance to me personally. To know that family and friends can trust me is high on my list. Equally so, to know that I can trust them is everything. I can love someone, enjoy their company, and yet close part of my heart to them because of a lack of trust. I felt that the Lord was bringing the importance of trust back full circle so that I would be aware of its value in my life and not close Him out.

I called Joanna and shared my realization of the importance of trust. I told her how I had seen Crystal as a gift from the Lord, not only to Victor and the family, but especially to me. Only to see Him take the gift back! It didn't seem right; you're not supposed to take back a gift!

Later that day, Joanna shared her thoughts on what I had told her earlier. My friend's words were like a balm; they comforted and eased the pain in my heart. She said,

> "As I thought about what you said about the gift and God taking it back, I was sad. But then I thought, what if it was the other way around. God knew the number of Crystal's days, her character, and her heart. He also knew the desires of her heart and the pain she had suffered growing up. What if the gift was to Crystal—to have a family who she knew

loved her with all their hearts and a man who adored her? What if the last four years were about blessing the end of her life. As I think about all the ways that God provided special favor and blessing on the wedding preparations, clearly, He was making her final days on earth as beautiful as they could be. Yes, Crystal was a gift to you, to Victor, and to all of you, but I think that you all were an even bigger gift to her. I think that God truly gave her the desire of her heart before He took her home—He used you to do that for her."

Chapter Thirteen

FORGIVENESS
And Slowness to Anger

God doesn't promise to save us from adversity, burdens, and crises in this life, but he does make us resilient people. He gives us his own qualities of unsinkability. We can bounce back. Even when we're floundering in the depths of difficulty, even when we think we're going under for the third time, there is prayer. There is forgiveness. There is waiting. There is hope.

—Robert J. Morgan[20]

IT WAS AUGUST 9, 2011, AND I woke up wanting to read the Bible. The thing is, I didn't even know where to start . . . I no sooner thought it and sensed, "Read what you are supposed to read." I knew instantly what that meant! I had just signed up for a class at Western Seminary, "Old Testament: Prophets, Interpreting Isaiah to Malachi." So, I went to my syllabus to see my first reading assignment—Nahum.

As I began to read the first chapter, I got emotional. "The Lord is slow to get angry, but his power is great, and he never lets the guilty go unpunished."[21] I cried out loud, "Lord, you must be angry over the death of Crystal! You may be slow to anger but this must make you angry. It should never have happened!! Your Word says that you never let the guilty go unpunished. So, I forgive them, but you go get them!! I want the men who are responsible for Crystal's death punished. I want them to be severely punished for the lies they've told, lies that Crystal and Victor cut their harness. Please, Lord, do not let the guilty go unpunished!!"

I paused a moment and continued reading, "The Lord is good, a strong refuge when trouble comes. He is close to those who trust in him."[22] I jotted down a few things in my journal,

Trouble has come, Lord, and I need your refuge! I am so devastated by Crystal's death. You say you are close to those who trust you. I want you close to me. I want to trust you! Help me to trust you!! I know I will never know why you allowed Crystal to die. I know there are secrets only you know.[23] I know you loved Crystal and I know you love me. I know you had to realize this would break my heart and devastate our whole family. I know you could have saved her, but you didn't. But you did save Victor's life. I know you are 100% powerful and I believe you are 100% loving and yet Crystal died. I hate even asking this, but you know it already, so I'm not hiding it from you. How can I fully trust you when you knew how much it would break our hearts and you let her die so young? Couldn't you have let us have her for a few more years? Couldn't you have let her be a mom? Couldn't you let us love her a little longer? I do trust you in so many ways. I want to trust you completely; I want to understand.

I've heard it said that when you hold onto anger, you become that anger. So much so that eventually it's all you are. But when you decide to let go of the anger and realize that sometimes the world is just an unjust place, you have another option. But, if you decide not to forgive, your life will be filled with anger, bitterness, and even hatred. So, I guess we must ask ourselves, "Which person do we want to become? Do we want to be that angry, bitter shell of a person?" I know I didn't want to be that person!

A few months after I had asked the Lord to "go get them," I had an encounter with Him. I was simply driving along, listening to music when the Holy Spirit whispered to me, "You don't even know these men." It hit me; I didn't know them. But I did know that they didn't set out for work on June 16 with the intention of a client dying. It was then that I started to grieve for these men. I even found myself praying that they would know they're forgiven. Next, I was asking the Lord to comfort them and give them peace.

I had started to soften some of my emotions since I made the decision that I didn't want anger to rule my life. Don't get me wrong, every emotion I felt was warranted in my grieving process, but I slowly let the anger step aside so that other sentiments had some space to surface. And I'm glad that I started this emotional journey when I did because it made way for some beautiful, bittersweet moments at Crystal's memorial.

Chapter Fourteen

CRYSTAL'S MEMORIAL
A Celebration and Such Great Sadness

Did you ever know, dear, how much you took away with
you when you left?
—C. S. Lewis [24]

AUGUST 15 WAS THE day that we gathered to celebrate the life of
our beloved Crystal. It was almost two months after the fateful day
of her death, and we came together to say our final goodbyes. As the
church filled, our family and close friends waited in the side rooms
together; awaiting the moment that would end a chapter in the story
of our lives. It was an important chapter . . . a beautiful chapter, and
it concluded far too soon.

As we entered the room and made our way to our seats, I realized
that there were several hundred people present. Their gaze was set on
us, but I had to look away. Seeing their grief, sorrow, and tears filled
my heart with immense pain and I was afraid that if I started crying,
I might not stop. Together, we were grieving the loss of a friendship
and a relationship that should have and could have been. We were
devastated by the fact that Crystal's death stopped her from making
her mark on the world. And I think we'd all agree that the world was
a better place when she was here and a lesser place now that she's gone.

Seventy-three days ago, Rob Maxey married Crystal and Victor
and now he stood before us again, but this time undertaking Crystal's

memorial. How can that be? It is still so surreal to me! Why? Just why? I keep asking that question over and over and yet no answer seems sufficient. No amount of wrestling can bring her back. So, for today, I lay my "why?" at the feet of Jesus. Though I'm left with questions and grief, I know she is not. I know that Crystal is now waiting for me in the very presence of God. No pain. No suffering. And, she has no unanswered questions. But here we are, paying tribute to Crystal—to who she was and who she will always be in our hearts. We loved her. She was part of our family. She truly had us at "hello" and to say we will miss her is such an understatement. She had such a zest for life and a smile that wouldn't quit, and we'll miss it greatly.

A close friend of Victor's opened the service as he read, "So with you: Now is your time of grief, but I will see you again and you will rejoice, and no one will take away your joy."[25] This is what keeps me going, even though Crystal's life was way too short, I know she is alive for eternity.

Following the reading, Mercy Me's "Homesick" played in the background as images of Crystal's life flashed across the screen. There were photos of her growing up, having fun, enjoying time with family and friends, laughing, and showing that amazing smile that always won everyone's heart. That's when the tears started to flow. As I looked at the pictures and listened to the words, I couldn't help but let emotions win out.

> *You're in a better place, I've heard a thousand times*
> *And at least a thousand times I've rejoiced for you*
> *But the reason why I'm broken, the reason why I cry*
> *Is how long must I wait to be with you*
>
> *I close my eyes and I see your face*
> *If home's where my heart is then I'm out of place*
> *Lord, won't you give me strength to make it through somehow*
> *I've never been more homesick than now*

Help me Lord cause I don't understand your ways
The reason why I wonder if I'll ever know
But, even if you showed me, the hurt would be the same
Cause I'm still here so far away from home

I close my eyes and I see your face
If home's where my heart is then I'm out of place
Lord, won't you give me strength to make it through somehow
I've never been more homesick than now

In Christ, there are no goodbyes
And in Christ, there is no end
So I'll hold onto Jesus with all that I have
To see you again
To see you again[26]

Sarah Spivey, Crystal's best friend from high school, gave her eulogy. She pointed out how Crystal had a knack for making new friends. She talked about how she was always friendly and welcomed people in with her beautiful smile. She shared about Crystal's love of soccer from an early age and that the love continued throughout high school and college. Crystal always had an extremely competitive spirit and wanted to be good at anything and everything she did. Sarah recalled a phone call from Crystal after one of her soccer games. Crystal had been so excited that she could barely get the words out: "I scored the winning header in my game!" Sarah thought back on how that conversation perfectly reflected Crystal—competitive and overcome with joy and excitement. Sarah also talked about some of Crystal's involvement in the National Honor Society and as a mathlete. She recalled their Algebra Two class and how everyone sat slouched in their seats. But not Crystal! She sat up straight with a huge smile on her face like it was her favorite place to be.

Sarah went on to talk about Crystal and her college days . . . She had always talked about going out of state and she landed on the University of New Mexico. Sarah relived those days as if they had just happened. She shared about how happy she was for Crystal but how sad she was that her friend would be so far away. She recalled the day that Crystal left; it was so bittersweet. Sarah, Crystal's Grandma Donna, her sister Taylor, and her brother Erik saw her off in a flood of tears. But New Mexico brought so many new experiences for Crystal and the chance to meet so many new people as well.

I knew where Sarah's story was headed, and I smiled softly as I thought about those early days between Victor and Crystal. Sarah shared about how she and Victor worked together at Mr. Pickles Sandwich Shop. And the first time Crystal came home to visit, Sarah talked endlessly about how excited she was. Sarah spoke so highly of Crystal that Victor finally said, "You should bring Crystal to the softball game tonight. The Mr. Pickles softball team is playing . . . I'll be playing . . . it would be fun if you guys came to watch." It took very little convincing because Crystal loved sports and so they went to the game. Victor was in the outfield when he saw Sarah walk up with someone he didn't know. He thought, "Man, I hope that's Sarah's friend Crystal!"

A few days later Crystal headed back to New Mexico. Later that week, Sarah and Victor were working together, and he quickly asked Sarah if he could have Crystal's number. Not even ten minutes later, Crystal texted Sarah asking for Victor's number. From that day on, they texted and talked constantly. When Crystal came home to visit on her winter break, Victor took her on their first date. They started dating shortly thereafter. Sarah even shared how Crystal was immediately welcomed into our family.

Sarah talked about how difficult the long-distance relationship was for them but how they made it look so easy. She recalled Crystal's semester abroad in Australia (on the one full scholarship that was offered!) and several other trips. She shared one of my favorite memories, too . . . After finishing up in Australia, Crystal flew to New York to attend Victor's cousin's wedding. That's where she met Rubén's family. The Rodriguez family also took Crystal to her first Broadway play, to Times Square, and even to New Jersey to meet Jeanne's side of the family. Both sides of Victor's family loved Crystal and told him he better marry that girl! We, of course, agreed!

Following that trip, Crystal returned to Sacramento to live near Victor, her family, and friends. She transferred to California State University where she was studying nursing. Sarah talked about Crystal and Victor's involvement in the church community, how they took a group of youth on a mission trip to Mexico, and lots of other little details about them serving together.

Since Victor loved playing indoor softball, Crystal began playing softball as well. She wasn't so hot at first, but with Crystal's competitive spirit, she quickly became a solid player. And when she hit her first home run, you can be sure that she did a little dance! Victor and Crystal became familiar faces out at the arena and, as you know, played on Down & Dirty together.

Sarah talked about the camping trip on the 4th of July weekend in 2010 . . . The one with their friends Chris and Dolly to Dillon Beach. And how he couldn't wait to propose on the fourth like he planned and instead proposed on July third . . . And Sarah couldn't talk about Victor and Crystal's engagement without mention of Crystal's crazy work ethic. At one point she had so many jobs—seven—that it was almost easier to ask where she *didn't* work! And, of course, that was seven jobs on top of going to school full time.

Sarah talked about the next eleven months in a few sweeping comments about wedding planning with Crystal and the Rodriguez family. The date was set for June 4, 2011. The location . . . outside! As you already know, that didn't work out the way we had planned. But as you also know, Crystal took the rain all in stride and made the most of the day and the moment. It was a joyous occasion and Sarah shared how she was so proud, happy, and delighted to be a part of it all. To see Crystal with her dream wedding with her dream guy was just so beautiful.

As Sarah closed, she read a note from Crystal's journal, "In this stressful day and age, it's nice to be excited about everyday things." Sarah suggested that if we want to celebrate Crystal, maybe we should all learn to smile a bit more, have an all-around positive attitude about life, and maybe do a little dance when we hit a home run.

After Sarah, Crystal's friend and University of New Mexico roommate, Brandy Price spoke. Brandy talked about how sincere and genuine Crystal was, and of her eagerness to learn and explore. She shared how every semester Crystal took one or two classes that weren't required simply because she wanted to learn something new. Her excitement to acquire knowledge truly inspired Brandy. In fact, Crystal's excitement for everything was an inspiration. She was genuinely excited to find an old penny on the sidewalk and equally so loved that olives fit perfectly well on the tips of her fingers. But her excitement didn't stop there, it also stretched to the people she loved. Brandy felt that Proverbs 17:17 best described their friendship, "A friend loves at all times."

She left us with these words, "When you think of Crystal, I want you to imagine a crisp morning; the sun just starting to peek over tall mountains, illuminating the hot air balloons in the west; or an afternoon thunderstorm, rain falling on the dry soil of the desert and giving the air that perfect smell of fresh earth, because Crystal loved those things."

Crystal's cousin Lena shared next. She talked about what an amazing young woman Crystal was . . . that she was outgoing, energetic, hardworking, competitive, and fearless. She spoke of her contagious laugh and that smile that lit up the room every time she walked in. Lena relived one of many memories: it was the first time she watched Crystal play soccer. Crystal was about twelve years old and absolutely loved playing soccer. And, as you can imagine, she was extremely passionate about it! At the end of the half, Crystal came off the field and very excitedly said, "Did you see that play?" Lena responded, "Was that legal?" to which Crystal responded, "Lena, it's only illegal if the ref sees it." We all laughed as we thought about little twelve-year-old Crystal.

Lena went on to share how she thought Crystal was the busiest person she knew. Between her numerous jobs, college classes, and sports, she was surprised that she found time to sleep. But even with her busy schedule, Crystal always found time for her brothers and sisters whom she loved so much. They were so important to her. Lena recalled that Crystal would watch her sister Taylor cheer and her brother Erik play sports. She would take her brother David to get his favorite cookies and her youngest sister Hailey out for ice cream. Crystal would even host sleepovers and take them all swimming. She was a wonderful big sister! In fact, Crystal loved *all* kids and wanted them all to succeed. She truly wanted the best for everyone. Crystal led by example and always tried to do the right thing. Lena wrapped up with these words: "I hope that all of us take away from this tragedy how precious life is and not to take any time for granted."

My son Kevin got up next. His words were bittersweet and particularly touched my heart. "I'm Kevin. I'm Crystal's brother-in-law, book buddy, and the guy who called her all the time to say, 'Hey Crystal, I need to talk to your boyfriend, can you put him on.'" Kevin went on to tell us the first time he realized she was part of the family . . . It was a couple of years before Victor and Crystal got married. The family was planning Kevin's birthday celebration and there were some scheduling conflicts, including one with Crystal. Kevin said, "I made the mistake of saying, 'Crystal isn't technically part of the family yet.'" He recollected that he received an intense glare from me and a quick reply, "Of course she is! Why would you say that?!" In the end, the plans worked out and everyone went to dinner. Kevin went on to tell us about the dinner and how the conversation turned to sports at one point. That's when Crystal leaned into him and said, "This conversation is probably boring you; is there a book you've read recently that you'd like to talk about?" "That's the moment I knew that Crystal was part of the family."

He continued saying that he was glad Brandy mentioned the penny. Every time he sees a penny, he thinks of Crystal. Without fail, she would get excited and say, "Oh, there's a penny on the ground!" One day when she did this, Kevin said, "Crystal, it's a penny, it has no value." That's when Crystal told him that it *did* have value, that it was her little reminder. She went on to tell him that every time she saw a penny, she liked to pick it up, look at it and read, "In God We Trust." And she would ask herself, "Am I trusting God?" Then she would feel good because she realized that she was, and everything was okay.

Kevin left us with these words, "Crystal made a great family even better. She made a great friendship the best. She has not left a hole for us, she left us memories and impact that will last forever for everyone who knew her."

Pastor Rob Maxey followed Kevin. As he approached the mic, he said, "I don't have all the answers, but I'd like to share Scripture to soak our hearts. There are no clever words and no great stories that could compare to God's truth." Rob shared about King David . . . how he was a man who was accustomed to tragedies and was also called a man after God's heart. He read Psalm 23, written by King David:

> *The LORD is my shepherd;*
> *I shall not want.*
> *He makes me to lie down in green pastures;*
> *He leads me beside the still waters.*
> *He restores my soul;*
> *He leads me in the paths of righteousness*
> *For His name's sake.*
> *Yea, though I walk through the valley of the shadow of death,*
> *I will fear no evil;*
> *For You are with me;*
> *Your rod and Your staff, they comfort me.*
> *You prepare a table before me in the presence of my enemies;*
> *You anoint my head with oil;*
> *My cup runs over.*
> *Surely goodness and mercy shall follow me*
> *All the days of my life;*
> *And I will dwell in the house of the LORD*
> *Forever.*[27]

Then he continued,

Now I saw a new heaven and a new earth, for the first heaven and the first earth had passed away. Also, there was no more sea. Then I, John, saw the holy city, New Jerusalem, coming down out of heaven from God, prepared as a bride adorned for her husband. And I heard a loud voice from heaven saying, 'Behold, the tabernacle of God is with men, and He will dwell with them, and they shall be His people. God Himself will be with them and be their God. And God will wipe away every tear from their eyes; there shall be no more death, nor sorrow, nor crying. There shall be no more pain, for the former things have passed away.' Then He who sat on the throne said, 'Behold, I make all things new.' And He said to me, 'Write, for these words are true and faithful.'[28]

Rob told us, as Christ followers, we need to be encouraged by these readings. He reminded us why we call this day a celebration of life because Crystal lived her short years to the fullest. Even with all of her jobs and going to school full time, she always had time for her family, for her friends, and to make new friends.

Rob recalled the first time he met Crystal . . . It was on a baseball field, and she was watching Victor coach his baseball team. He shared how she was chatty and so proud of Victor. He could tell that she was his biggest fan. Rob pointed out, despite how busy she was, when she sat with you, she made you feel that you were the only one she cared about. She had that unique ability.

Rob's demeanor changed; he took a deep breath and told us that he remembered getting the call about the accident. He got in his car and started driving to our house but was overcome with anger, confusion, and frustration. He knew people wanted answers and he didn't have any. Rob reminded us that we can be frustrated . . . that we can yell at God . . . that we can just vent to God. He is capable and able to take our frustration, our disappointment, our anger, our confusion, and over time, through His Holy Spirit, begin to soften our hearts and allow us to move forward. Rob gently reminded us how Crystal was solid in her faith and as the song stated,

> *In Christ, there are no goodbyes*
> *And in Christ, there is no end*
> *So I'll hold onto Jesus with all that I have*
> *To see you again*
> *To see you again*[29]

Rob then blessed us with his parting words: "May the God of hope fill you all with all joy and peace in believing, so that by the power of the Holy Spirit you may abound in hope."[30]

With her beautiful voice and sweet piano playing, Karla Webb led us in "Amazing Grace." Then Jeanie Scott Coca, a dear friend of Victor's from high school, shared "A Grateful Heart—In Crystal's Own Words." We had given her all of Crystal's journals, including her gratitude journal and asked her to summarize Crystal's thoughts.

Jeanie told us, "If you were blessed to know Crystal, you know that her happiness was anything but artificial or forced. It was real, natural, and extremely contagious. And that's because her happiness came from her heart, a heart that loved life and a heart that was truly grateful for what she had been given. Whether times were good or bad, hard or easy, she had a gift for making the best of it and radiating true happiness."

At the end of high school and into college, Crystal journaled about her gratitude for various aspects of her life that brought her joy. Just as Crystal's presence brought us joy and laughter, Jeanie hoped her words would bring a smile to our faces and a sparkle of happiness to our lives.

In various entries of her journal, Crystal showed how much she enjoyed the simple things in life. She writes,

> *I am grateful that I enjoy watching sports, and that I am a good proofreader for papers.*

> *I'm grateful that on this women's retreat I have a comfy sleeping bag.*

I'm grateful for soccer because it makes me happy, and I love it!

I'm grateful for my straight teeth because I love to smile, and I'm grateful for smiling, I think it's the most amazing way to communicate to people, whether or not they speak the same language.

Crystal also expressed how thankful she was that her personality had a good influence on other people. She shares,

I am grateful for the joy that I bring to others. Thanks, God, for giving me that gift.

I am thankful for the gift of laughter, and I am so glad I can laugh at myself when funny things happen.

I am also grateful for having two hands and two feet that allow me to work. And I am glad that I am enthusiastic because it makes me and everyone else around me happy!

In addition to her enjoyment of life and laughter, Crystal filled her journal with gratitude for many of her friends and family members. In some of her entries she says,

I am grateful for all the people in my life who love me and who want to see me succeed.

I am grateful for new friends like Shawna and Sydnie.

I am thankful for my siblings, and I am thankful for time with my family.

I am thankful for Brandy making me a workout plan.

I am grateful for every day I get to spend with my grandma.

I am so thankful for Victor's amazing family, and I am grateful for Victor's mom Jeanne because she always thinks of me no matter what she is doing.

I'm thankful for Sarah because she is always there when I need her, and I'm thankful for the Falkenstein's because I have learned so much from them.

> *I am grateful for my sister Taylor and how much I love to hang out with her.*
>
> *I am always grateful for the support I've received from all of my friends and family!*

Throughout her journal, Crystal also made it clear that her happiness and gratitude came from a true faith in Jesus Christ. Her journal is covered in prayers and praises to her Lord. In several prayers, she writes,

> *I am thankful to have an intimate and personal relationship with my Lord and Savior Jesus Christ.*
>
> *I am thankful that we don't have to be perfect or worry about our sins because of the infinite forgiveness you give. Also, I thank you for giving your only Son to die on the cross for all the sins we commit, Lord. I love worship music, and I love you, Father.*
>
> *I am grateful I have you God and I'm thankful that you are a God of hope. Thank you for the peace of mind I get by knowing that everything happens for a reason, and all the plans you have for me are good.*

And more than anything, Crystal always wrote about God's greatest blessing in her life, Victor—He was her one love and her best friend. This is beautifully expressed in her journal as anyone can tell from just these few entries. Crystal writes,

> *Only you, Lord, could have brought me someone so perfect for me, and I thank you immensely for that. I know and can feel it now that he is part of your plan for me!*
>
> *I am thankful for my friendship with Victor. He brings me true joy.*
>
> *I am grateful for Victor's humor and how much he makes me laugh.*
>
> *I am grateful for how happy Victor makes me and how goofy he can be.*
>
> *I am grateful for Victor making me smile every single day!*

I am thankful for the special time I get to have with him, even when it is just watching a silly TV show.

I am thankful for having someone like Victor who will hold and console me when everything doesn't go my way. He's so amazing and he treats me like a princess. I know he loves me more than anyone on this earth ever could.

Finally, in one of her most sincere journal entries, Crystal states her greatest hope: "My ultimate goal in life is not to get rich or become famous or anything artificial like that, my goal is to have a good family." Crystal got it right, and the Lord blessed her with the desire of her heart. She truly valued what really matters in life and her perspective on life serves as an inspiration and encouragement to all of us. Through her love and gratitude for life, Crystal will forever be a precious gift of pure happiness and joy to our hearts.

The memorial ended in prayer and countless people came up to our family to extend their condolences. Some wanted to share stories about Crystal. Others just wanted to hug our necks and love on us. I'm thankful there was time and space for all of it. There was such an outpouring of love and compassion, and it filled my heart.

A week after the service, I was reading one of the Psalms and tears just began cascading down my cheeks. After a few moments, I felt led to read Psalm 116. I dismissed it for the moment and continued reading the passage that I was in. The prompting wouldn't go away so I finally turned to Psalm 116 and started reading. "I love the LORD, for he heard my voice; he heard my cry for mercy. Because he turned his ear to me, I will call on him as long as I live."[31] Then I came to verse 15, "Precious in the sight of the Lord is the death of His saints."[32] Once again, the Lord reminded me that despite my sorrows, Crystal was genuinely delighted because she was with Him and in His presence for all of eternity. I just wish *that* truth would align with my heart. I wish my heart wasn't so heavy with such deep sorrow. Grief demands an answer, but sometimes there is no answer.

Chapter Fifteen

MY DARKEST MOMENT
When Hope First Met Hopelessness

*When we honestly ask ourselves which person in our lives
mean the most to us, we often find that it is those who,
instead of giving advice, solutions, or cures, have chosen
rather to share our pain and touch our wounds with a
warm and tender hand. The friend who can be silent with
us in a moment of despair or confusion, who can stay with
us in an hour of grief and bereavement, who can tolerate
not knowing, not curing, not healing and face with us the
reality of our powerlessness, that is a friend who cares.*

—Henri Nouwen[33]

AFTER BEING IN THE hospitals for almost six weeks, Victor was
finally home with us, but it was short lived. He decided to move out not
long after being released because there were just too many memories
of Crystal in our home. We were all just trying to figure out how to
go on in the day-to-day of life without Crystal. Following her memorial, however, it seemed as if life was business as usual for everyone . . .
everyone except our family. We were still very much dealing with the
catastrophic loss of Crystal.

There comes a time in all our lives when reality hits—getting
another job isn't going to happen quickly . . . you really are going to
lose your house . . . the divorce is going to happen . . . there won't be

a reconciliation . . . the one you love isn't going to walk through the door ever again. That's what happened to me . . . that last reality hit, and it hit hard.

It was late one evening and I was home alone. Rubén was working the night shift and Victor was living with friends. I was downstairs sitting on the couch in the dark. The wind was whipping around outside, and it was pouring down rain. As I sat there in the silence, the strong winds rattled the front door so hard that it made me look over at it. That's when it hit me. It hit me like a tsunami . . . Crystal was never going to walk through that door again. She was never coming home. Tears welled up in my eyes and I just sat there and wept. I never saw that moment coming and honestly, most of us don't see them coming, those moments that'll bring the best cry and the deepest longing for our loved ones.

The loss of Crystal was so overwhelming; she had filled a space in my heart that I never knew was empty. My suffering was just so unbearable. I had never felt such pain, not only in my heart but literally throughout my whole body. I physically hurt as I grieved her loss. And as I sat there, weeping turned to sobs and my sobs to a guttural cry as I wailed out to God, "Will I ever be able to smile again? Will I ever be happy? Will I ever have joy in my life?"

Right after I cried out to the Lord, my phone vibrated. Who was texting me at 10:00 PM?! I picked up my phone, wiped the tears away to clear my sight and saw this text from my friend Cathy Yanez. She said, "I have been praying all weekend for Victor—but the Lord wants me to pray for you **now**."

I sat there for a moment just processing what was happening. Cathy was praying for me because the Lord put me on her heart. The God to whom I just cried out was already looking out for me. The God of the Universe, the Creator of the heavens, The Almighty put me on a friend's heart in my greatest moment of need. In an instant, I sensed the Lord saying to me, "I see you. I see your brokenness. I care and I love you!" It was then that hope met hopelessness. That's when

God met me. It was just the beginning . . . I wasn't full of hope, but it was starting, and I was comforted.

During this tremendous time of grief, I appreciated more than ever before prayers over my family and me. For the first time, I was aware of how the power of prayer had carried me through this time of sorrow. There was also such an overwhelming sense of how much I not only needed the Lord, but how important it was for me to hear from Him and sense His closeness . . . And I did! I believe that the Word of God is true; I always have. But, in this season, certain Scriptures became real in a way they never had before. One was, "The LORD is close to the brokenhearted and saves those who are crushed in spirit."[34]

I have never felt such closeness to the Lord than during those times. And even though I still grapple with the death of Crystal—not understanding why the Lord allowed it—I am aware of how my love for Him has increased.

Chapter Sixteen

A JOB CHANGE

The Fork in the Road

Don't be afraid of change. You may lose something good, but
you may gain something better.

—Author Unknown

I LEFT FOR THE Bahamas on June 17, 2011. After two weeks had passed, with no indication of when we would be able to bring our son home, my boss hired someone to do my job. I worked in Women's Ministry, and they found someone to step in when I wasn't in a position to return to ministry just yet. This was a temporary position and what I believed a creative solution to an unforeseen situation.

Ten days after the memorial, I had a meeting with my boss and my director. They both expressed their sorrow for my loss and told me that they knew the Lord was going to use me. "Jeanne," they said, "just think . . . you can minister even more to women now. And maybe even write a book!" My head was spinning and everything inside me was screaming, "Are you kidding me?! What are you talking about me ministering to women? My heart feels like it's bleeding it hurts so bad! And no, I don't want to write a book!!" Thankfully, my exterior and interior didn't mirror each other. I politely smiled and listened.

They talked about my ministry opportunities for a bit longer and then circled back to the real point of the meeting, "Jeanne, are you planning to come back to work?" they asked in unison. After a moment,

I responded, "Well, I was thinking about coming back on September 6th." They smiled and my boss replied, "I know your passion is speaking to women and I feel that the Lord is going to give you a platform . . . I want you to know that I'm your advocate, but things here at work are even faster paced than when you left. Maybe you should wait until October, after all of the Bible Studies have started."

As I pondered it, and before I could respond, she threw me a curveball, "Jeanne, if you were to return, we will need to change your work schedule. We need you to work Monday—Thursday, 9:00 AM–3:00 PM." What she said wasn't really registering until she continued, "I know—your Thursday morning Bible study is your lifeline, but we need to do this." Before I even knew what was happening, tears were flowing down my cheeks, and I had no control over them. She was right, my Thursday morning Bible study was a lifeline. We had been together for over twelve years, and I've known these women for more than twenty-five. And that's not even taking into account everything they've done for me with the loss of Crystal . . . I was so angry and so disappointed in their decision to change my hours. How could they do this knowing that I just lost Crystal? I politely responded, "I'll think about it and discuss it with Rubén."

They knew that I was taking a little getaway trip for a few days at Mount Hermon. It's a beautiful center in the Santa Cruz mountains that's available for camps and personal retreats. They wanted me to pray about everything and let them know my decision when I returned. I told them that I would hold off on coming back in September but would most likely return in October.

I was so upset; so livid! How could they do this to me?! I drove home in a storm of emotions. As I walked through the front door of our home, tears streaming down my cheeks, I told Rubén everything. He's a practical man. What I mean is that he can remove emotions from the situation, and I clearly couldn't do that at the time. That's when he gently replied, "Jeanne, you can't be angry; your boss is just telling you what she needs. I understand the importance of your Bible study, especially during this time, so if you feel you need to quit, we will just readjust our budget." I was so relieved by Rubén's response and felt a burden lift. But it was a fork in the road, and I needed to decide which path to take.

The day of my getaway was finally here! But first I had breakfast with my friend Joanna. I told her what happened and expressed to her that I hated that I even had to think about this right now. "I've decided I'm not putting any more stress on myself, Joanna. I have enough going on, so I'm staying unless I hear otherwise from the Lord. Even if I miss hearing the Lord telling me that I'm supposed to leave, I know I will eventually hear Him, and I can always leave later."

Then my friend said something very profound, "You know when I am waiting on the Lord for direction, I don't usually tell Him what I'm going to do. I don't know what the right thing is, but I really think that this is the time for seeking and listening." I was humbled by her response and saddened by mine.

Looking back, I can say that in this season, I was struggling with grief, anger, and confusion. I had enough going on and I didn't want to make a career change on top of everything else at that point in my life. My intention wasn't necessarily to make the decision but rather to keep things status quo. And, if I heard anything from the Lord about leaving, then I would be obedient.

Chapter Seventeen

TIME TO GET AWAY

A Voice in the Darkness

In our sleep, pain which cannot forget falls drop by drop
upon the heart until, in our own despair, against our will,
comes wisdom through the awful grace of God.

—Aeschylus

A FRIEND'S DAUGHTER MADE it possible for me to have this weekend away at Mount Hermon. It was a chance to be alone with the Lord to process all that happened to my family and to me. As I made the almost-three-hour drive, I was listening to some worship music. I'd occasionally have to switch over to talk radio because the songs would touch my heart so much that I'd start crying and couldn't see the road. One of those times that I switched over to the radio, the talk show host was discussing a new study that was completed in Florida. Through this research, they found that a good cry doesn't relieve stress . . . that you need a person to talk to for that to happen. I thought, "Great, I had planned on having some good cries and now they say it's better to have someone to talk to!" Then I sensed God whisper to me, "You do have someone to talk to . . . you have Me."

After I checked in and got settled, I took my CD player with my favorite songs, and I went for a walk. I came to a bridge and began to cross it. When I was halfway across, I stopped and looked down at the stream below. As I stood there for a bit, listening to one of the songs,

I realized that tears were running down my face as fast as the stream was moving below. The words were touching the depths of my soul:

I'm on my knees, Father, will you turn to me?
Could the maker of the stars hear the sound of my
breaking heart?
If you're everything you say you are, would you come close to
hold my heart?[35]

I stood there and pondered the words a while. Then I started talking with God. I told Him that I believed His promises remain true even though I didn't understand why it all happened. Among other things, I told Him how much I needed Him to fill the void in my heart that Crystal had left.

Later that night, I was on my knees sobbing into a huge towel because tissues couldn't handle the tears that were pouring from my eyes. Everything that had transpired came crashing down and we finally landed on my job. I said, "Lord, I don't even want to think about the job. Can I just give it to You?" I sensed His response, and these words came to me, "Have I not always directed your path?" I just had to smile and out loud replied, "Yes!"

Shortly after I responded, I was prompted to read about Moses, so I got up, grabbed my Bible, and turned to the book of Exodus. The passage said that the people moved when the cloud moved and as I read it, I heard the Lord tell me that when He moves, I was to move. I started thinking through what that could mean . . . Does that mean I'm supposed to move away from my job? Or am I supposed to move away from my Bible study? I burst out loud again, "It's my lifeline, God! I can't!" And He quickly whispered, "I am your lifeline." He was right but that didn't make it any less hard. Out of complete faith, I replied, "Lord, I'll do whatever You want me to do and go wherever You want me to go."

The next day I was reading a verse from Proverbs, "Trust in the Lord with all your heart and lean not on your own understanding."[36]

I found myself telling the Lord that His ways are sometimes hard to understand but I knew I needed to:

- Trust Him when my questions aren't answered.
- Trust Him when I don't understand.
- Trust His Heart.
- Trust His Purpose.
- Trust Him when my heart is broken.
- Trust His goodness.
- Trust that He knows best.
- Trust that His plans are bigger than mine.
- Trust that He will keep His word.
- Trust that He will be enough.
- Trust Him . . . and Him alone!!

And as much as I *know* I need to trust, I still had to ask God to help me to trust Him!

On Sunday morning, as I was doing my last devotional, everything I had experienced with the Lord came together as I read this quote from Joni Erickson Tada, "Faith isn't the ability to believe long and far into the misty future. It's simply taking God at His Word and taking the next step."[37]

Chapter Eighteen

WHAT NOW?

And the Cloud Moves

O Lord, hear my prayer, listen to my cry for mercy; in your faithfulness and righteousness come to my relief.

Psalm 143:1 [38]

ON SEPTEMBER 22, I HAD a follow-up meeting with my boss. Instead of my director, someone from HR (Human Resource) was present as well. I thought it odd but figured it had something to do with the change in my schedule. As we got started, my boss asked, "So, how are you feeling?" I enthusiastically replied, "I'm doing great and I'm really looking forward to coming back on October 3rd." She stopped me before I could go any further. "So, that's what I want to talk to you about. We want you to come back but we have a different proposal to offer you. As I mentioned before, some things around here have really increased in pace and intensity. We think a better fit for you is a receptionist job at the front . . ." I was still listening but kind of surprised about the new offer. She continued, ". . . To be on the phones . . . be a receptionist . . . welcome everybody in with your warmth and friendliness . . . and still be in community with us right here in this building." My mind was beginning to drift and starting to ask questions. She went on to tell me that she talked to HR about my Thursday Bible study and how important it is, how it's my lifeline . . . She told them that Women's Ministry couldn't offer me Thursday mornings off but hoped the receptionist position would. She concluded with, "Jeanne, I really do feel that the receptionist position would be a better fit for you."

Thinking there were still two offers on the table, I told them that it was enticing but I was prepared to come back and work Monday through Thursday, 9:00 AM–3:00 PM. My boss jumped in, "So, I guess I'm confused . . . with me, the position is Monday through Thursday and you'd come back for that and miss your Bible study, but with this new offer, you're hesitating?" She just couldn't understand why I would come back and miss my Bible study when I could take the receptionist job and be able to go to my study. Then it all came out. "So, this is the conversation I had with HR and that's why I've asked them to be here . . . This is the job they are offering you." I paused for a moment and replied, "Okay, so what I'm hearing you say is my current job is NOT being offered." "Yes," she replied. I knew then that the cloud had moved.

I had been diligently asking the Lord to show me what I needed to do and to make it plain to me. Well, I don't think He could have made it any plainer: my job was not there for me to have. The cloud had *definitely* moved. Yes, I was hurt and angry and yet blessed that the Lord prepared me. Whether or not it was right or fair, it doesn't matter. God allowed it. So, I looked forward to a new day with this verse in the forefront of my mind, "If God is for us who can be against us?"[39] And I knew that God was for me!

I will always be involved in women's lives; this is not only my call but my heart. A job title doesn't make me who I am; I don't have to work in Women's Ministry to minister to women. I ended up taking the receptionist job. As I signed the paperwork, I asked our HR Rep if he knew why my job wasn't being offered. I wanted to learn and grow from this experience. And God gave me a little smile of affirmation when the HR Rep replied, "I have had no idea why but I'm so happy that you're staying on. I've only heard good things about you, Jeanne."

Chapter Nineteen

MY ENCOUNTER WITH GOD

And the Question I Had to Answer

When you survive loss . . . everyone is quick to tell you how
strong you are, and how tough you must be. But actu-
ally, no one has a choice to survive grief do they . . . it's not
optional. You just have to cry in the shower, sob in your
pillow and pray you will make it.

—Zoe Clark-Coates[40]

ALMOST A YEAR LATER, I went to a conference with my friend
Joanna. Before it started, she asked me if I was mad at God. Kind of
surprised, I said, "I have no right to be mad because of all the things
God has done for my family." She stopped me right there and said, "That
doesn't answer the question . . ." Well, I never actually answered that question. I was saved by the bell, I guess, because the conference started before
I could. But I did continue to think about her question and realized that
I *was* angry with God. But I didn't want to deal with it . . . I didn't want
to be angry with anyone I love and that I know loves me, especially God!
I've heard it said, "What lies behind us and what lies before us are tiny
matters compared to what lies within us."[41] I knew if I kept holding onto
my anger that eventually it would take hold of me and take over. That's
not who I wanted to become—an angry, bitter person!

A few weeks later, I drove up to Lake Tahoe for a retreat with my
Thursday morning Bible study, we call ourselves the Calendar Girls.

That first night I shared with them that I was angry at God. My friend Suzanne Delfin chuckled and said, "Jeanne, God *knows* that you're angry at Him and it's time for you to sit with Him and tell Him instead of holding it in." She wasn't wrong but I just didn't quite know what to do with that.

The next morning everyone went to take a hike, which left me alone at the cabin. After they left, I got out my Bible and started reading Psalm 138, "Though I walk in the midst of trouble, you preserve my life . . . your right hand delivers me."[42] I stopped and just started crying. I was in trouble. My life was in a storm, and I was out of control in so many different areas of my life. But then I continued, "The Lord will fulfill his purpose for me; your steadfast love, O Lord, endures forever. Do not forsake the work of your hands."[43] The tears continued! Now they were tears of solace; it was comforting to know that even though I was going through this time of struggle, pain, and anger, His Word tells me that He will fulfill His purpose for me!

As I read Psalm 139, the Lord made it so clear that He knows everything about me, right down to when I sit and when I rise. He even knows my thoughts from afar.[44] After I finished that chapter, I walked out to the deck, sat down, and looked at the splendor of Lake Tahoe. In that moment, I recognized that *He* created it all and I thanked Him for it.

I was finally being honest with God. I was angry with Him. As I sat there, tears running down my face (my nose running, too), I was so mad and so hurt. I questioned God. I challenged God. I felt like Job in the Bible when he said, "My days are over. My hopes have disappeared. My heart's desires are broken."[45] And like Job, I had so many questions. With anger in my voice and tears flooding my eyes, I cried out, "WHY? WHY DID YOU LET THIS HAPPEN? WHY? When you knew this would break my heart! WHY DID YOU ALLOW THIS WHEN YOU KNEW THAT THIS WOULD DEVASTATE OUR WHOLE FAMILY! WHY couldn't you let us love her a little longer? WHY couldn't you let her be a wife a few more years? WHY didn't you let us enjoy them as a married couple? WHY couldn't you have let her be a mom? WHY didn't you save her? WHY? WHY? WHY?"

I told God how much I loved Crystal and it was then that it hit me why I was so incredibly angry. God put Crystal in my life, and I opened my heart wide open. There are only a small handful of people to whom I have opened my heart that wide, and Crystal was one of them. Now she was gone, and the pain was so incredibly excruciating. I was furious because I loved her so much and now, because of that great love, I was in tremendous pain. I was not only feeling my own pain but the pain of Victor and the suffering he was feeling from the loss of the one he loved. And then there's the pain of Kevin struggling with Crystal's death, and of course Rubén and everything he's working through . . . It was too much pain all the way around.

And when I had no more questions and no more tears left, I sat before the Lord in silence. In the end, God didn't give me answers to any of my questions. But like Job, He asked me a question instead. With a father's tender heart, He said to me, "Would you rather not have loved her at all?" When that question came, I just let out a long sigh. I realized right then that God could have made that possible. Not to have known Crystal would have meant I wouldn't be in pain. I pondered the question for a while, "Would you rather not have loved her at all?" I found myself answering, "Of course not! Crystal was the daughter we never had. As much as she needed to be loved by us, we needed to be loved by her. Her ultimate goal in life was to have a good family and we were that family to her. We not only loved her; she knew we loved her."

Even before they were engaged, we included Crystal in our family pictures, family vacations (NYC, Disneyland, San Francisco . . .) and so many family memories—from breakfast with Rubén to movies and comic books with Kevin to restaurants and women's retreats with me. We needed Crystal as much as she needed us in her life. Not to have had a chance to love her, I would have been less of a person. And even though I walked away without answers to my questions, I knew that God loved me so much that He put Crystal in my life. How can I be angry for that?

Chapter Twenty

FINDING HOPE

The Choice is Up to You

Hope is being able to see that there is light despite all of the darkness.

—Desmond Tutu [46]

WE ALL HAVE HOPES—GETTING married, having children, grandchildren, being valued, losing weight, going on our dream vacation, making more money, buying a home, buying a new car, going to college, sending our child to college, living a long and prosperous life ...

I had hopes. I was finally seeing some of them come about and then in an instant, they were shattered. When Victor and Crystal got married, it was one of our family's happiest moments and then just twelve days later, it plunged into the darkest of times.

Crystal was not only the love of Victor's life, but she loved us like parents, and she genuinely loved our oldest son like a brother. We talked about future vacations together and watching the grandbabies when they had children. We had so many plans and so much hope for the future.

So, when our *hopes* don't happen, how do we wrap our brain around the verse in Romans that says, "Hope does not disappoint us."[47] Honestly, I don't know, but when Crystal died, I was definitely disappointed and full of despair. I felt like all my hopes died when she died. So, how can the Bible say, "Hope doesn't disappoint?" I grappled with a lot of things following Crystal's death. This was one of those things. I mean, how does hope not disappoint when a life is cut short, and dreams are lost forever?

My heart was shattered, and my hopes dashed. But then one day my friend Bonnie Koons emailed me these words, "I don't think a broken heart ever mends . . . I think it is always there but in time it is covered over like a soft blanket of snow, by the grace of God, so the pain is not so intense. I think that seasons come and go, and our lives get distracted and busy by a lot of things, so we can go on, but every once in a while, the wind blows and exposes that, what has been covered over, and once again, we feel the pain, cry, and relive the loss as well as all the beautiful memories that we had. And just when we feel we can't go on, that soft blanket of snow blows in again, like the Balm of Gilead, and life continues with Him who is our Hope."

So, what does hope do for us? When I think about that question, I remember something my friend Joanna said, "I know that the whole concept of hope must seem so abstract and almost wrong, and yet I genuinely believe that hope is the gift that God gives to show us ultimately a way to see through the pain and into the future that He has planned for us. I don't have a clue what that looks like, but I'm so grateful that He does."

So, I guess the question I'm asking is, how can we hold onto hope? How does hope not disappoint . . . and why?

I was still struggling with the hopes we had and how those hopes had died, changing our lives forever. But then I hit a real turning point. I was talking to Joanna about these things, and she said, "Be careful not to confuse the hopes with the person. Crystal is gone from your life and with her went many specific hopes and dreams. But don't confuse the hope with Crystal." She was so right! I had associated my hopes with Crystal, and I couldn't seem to separate the two. And when Joanna went on to say, "Hope is looking ahead," I realized that I was not entirely ready to do that. She reminded me, "For right now, that hope has a face." She was right again; my hope did have a face and that face was Crystal. But that's when I recognized I had it wrong . . . the face of hope is Jesus, not Crystal!

I know, I should have seen that coming but when you're grieving a loss, everything gets all twisted together. I truly started to understand hope as I read this passage, "May the God of **hope** fill you with all joy and peace as you trust in him, so that you may overflow with hope by the power of the Holy Spirit."[48] That brought me back to, "Now hope does not disappoint." But then I continued reading and discovered, "Because the love of God has been poured out in our hearts by the Holy Spirit who was given to us.[49]

Why did I feel disappointed when the Bible tells me that hope does not disappoint? Maybe it's because my brain was askew of what I thought hope was . . . how I defined hope as worldly happiness when it really meant hope in Jesus! So, maybe that's what it means in Isaiah when he writes, "Then you will know that I am the LORD; those who hope in me will not be disappointed."[50]

So, if my hopes and dreams were in Crystal and she died, then they died, too. In the beginning of my grief, I felt like Job when he said, "My days are over. My hopes have disappeared. My heart's desires are broken."[51] But when I realized that my true hope was in the person of Jesus Christ, then I saw hope differently. Don't get me wrong, I was still grieving and processing and learning, but I was starting to understand a bit more about true hope and how to uncover it. Some other verses that helped me in this process are:

"But now, Lord, what do I look for? My hope is in you."[52]

"Find rest, O my soul, in God alone; my hope comes from him."[53]

". . . A faith and knowledge resting on the hope of eternal life, which God, who does not lie, promised before the beginning of time . . ."[54]

It is true that the more I get to know Christ, the more I love Him. And the more I get to know Him, the more we have sweet moments together. Throughout my healing journey, I walked quite a bit to clear my head. At times, I would be covered with the intensity of God's love, so much so that I didn't know what to do. On one of those walks, the morning after Thriving Women's Conference, I thought of the times that Crystal and I went together. Of course, I started to cry. I knew she would have been with me that weekend; I would have loved on her, and she would have enjoyed being with my friends and me. A deep sense of loss was flooding over me. I just missed my daughter and my friend. As I was crying, God's love came over me. It was so intense that I had to stop walking. It was overwhelming and I could hardly breathe. Then it occurred to me, Crystal is with the Lord, and she's covered by His incredible love. As much as Victor loved her . . .and as much as I loved her . . . and as much her family and friends loved her . . . that was only a taste of how much God is loving on her right now! And I thought, "Wow, she deserves to be loved that much."

I knew at that moment, that I was starting to see hope through God's eyes! I have come to understand that I simply do not see the bigger picture, but I *choose* to put my hope in the Lord, and His bigger picture.

I do trust the Lord, that His ways are higher than mine. I know just how much He loves me and just how much he loves my family. It gives me great peace in knowing that I will see Crystal one day and that we will be in eternity together worshiping our Lord.

Chapter Twenty-one

LIFE AFTER CRYSTAL

Making My Darkest Hour, My Defining Moment

*I am always saddened by the death of a good person. It is
from this sadness that a feeling of gratitude emerges. I feel
honored to have known them and blessed that their passing
serves as a reminder to me that my time on this beautiful
earth is limited and that I should seize the opportunity
I have to forgive, share, explore, and love. I can think of no
greater way to honor the deceased than to live this way.*

—Steve Maraboli[55]

THEY SAY THAT TIME heals all wounds. That's not true! I found
that it was through the grace and mercy of the Lord that my wounds
were healed. I still have a nasty scar and it will forever be there, but
the intense pain has ceased. There are still times when I hear a song
or go somewhere that reminds me of Crystal and I find a tear or two
rolling down my cheeks, but the days of never-ending tears, intense
sorrow and excruciating pain are behind me.

I recognize that I can't trust God that my worst fear won't happen,
but I *can* trust God that He will be there for me regardless. Just like
I didn't want to let anger rule, I also don't want my wounds to make
me become someone that I'm not.

Crystal has gone on to be with the Lord; this will not change.
This is our new life, a life without her. It's a new chapter and a new

story—a chapter I never wanted and a story I would have never written for my family. But it is the story the Lord has allowed to be written. I don't want to walk around angry. Sometimes there are things we don't want to happen but must accept. Things we don't want to know but must learn . . . people we can't live without but must let go. My greatest spiritual growth has come from my deepest pain, and I had to accept that there are things that only God knows, and I need to trust Him that He will take care of what I don't understand.

Throughout that first year of grief and loss, I grappled with so many questions:

- What will I do? How will I respond?
- Will I let this great sadness take over my life?
- Do I trust in the Lord and put my hope in Him?
- Do I continue to praise Him, my Savior and my God?

There are so many things I will miss, so many things that I loved about Crystal:

- Her smile
- Her beautiful eyes
- Kissing her head
- Talking to her
- Going to our favorite restaurant, Danielle's
- Working with her at Macy's
- Seeing her sit on the couch doing homework
- Going to retreats with her
- Going on vacation with her and Victor
- Watching American Idol with her
- I loved that she considered Kevin her brother and she saw us as the parents she never had
- I loved how she went out to breakfast/lunch with just Rubén
- I loved that she was a reader like me
- I loved that she was frugal
- I loved that she was a hard worker
- I loved when she helped me cater parties

- I loved that she was ambitious
- I loved that she loved children
- I loved when she and Victor cooked for us
- I loved watching her play softball
- I loved that she went on a mission trip with Victor, and it touched her heart
- I loved that she received a full scholarship to study abroad for a semester in Australia
- I loved that she would ask us for advice and listened
- **I loved her!**

I am thankful for my years spent with Crystal, for the time and experiences we shared and everything I learned from her. She touched our lives so much; she filled a spot in our hearts that was just waiting for her. We will never be the same; we will be changed forever because Crystal came into our lives.

After the loss of Crystal, I remember thinking that I wasn't going to make it. And I never would have thought I could ever say, "I am so thankful for where I am." But I can tell you that God has been so good to me over the years. It's been hard but it's been beautiful, too.

Crystal's life ended too quickly but she will forever remain in our hearts and minds. But we get to choose how we will respond to adversities in our lives. I stumbled across these words somewhere and they just rang true:

> We can shed tears that our loved ones are gone, or we can smile because they lived.
> We can close our eyes and pray that they'll come back, or we can open our eyes and see all that they have left.
> Our hearts can be empty because we can't see them, or we can be full of the love that they shared.
> We can turn our backs on tomorrow and live in yesterday, or we can be happy for tomorrow because of yesterday.

We can remember them and that they have gone, or we can cherish their memory and let it live on.
We can try and close our minds, be empty and turn our backs, or we can do what they would want; smile, open our eyes, love, and go on.[56]

We can let our loss knock us out cold, we can drown in our misery, or we can choose to make our darkest hour our defining moment. We can choose to take something terrible and turn it into something good. I lived the heaviness. I felt all the feelings and all the emotions, but in the end, I chose hope over despair. I could have easily turned either way. I hope that my story and my openness will allow you to look at both sides of the situation and that you, too, will give hope a chance.

Chapter Twenty-two

THE CRYSTAL RODRIGUEZ MEMORIAL SCHOLARSHIP FUND (CRMSF)

Crystal's Legacy Lives On

So long as the memory of certain beloved friends lives in my heart, I shall say that life is good.

—Helen Keller

AFTER THE DEATH OF Crystal, Victor wanted to honor the memory of his deceased wife. Crystal loved school and because of scholarships, she was able to go to college. So, Victor decided that was what he wanted to do—to give scholarships to deserving students who wanted to further their education but needed some financial assistance. As a result, in September 2012, The Crystal Rodriguez Memorial Scholarship Fund (CRMSF) was established.

Victor asked their closest friends, Rubén, and me to be a part of this project. CRMSF is managed by a Board of Directors that is comprised of ten volunteer members with Victor as the president. The first meeting was held in our house to discuss how we would go about raising money for the scholarships. Since many of the board members played golf, they thought a golf tournament would be a good way to raise funds. Initially, I presumed they were talking about doing the tournament in 2013, giving us time to plan. But they wanted to do it right away so that we could give scholarships in school year 2012–2013.

Two months after that initial meeting, on a bitter cold November morning, we had thirty-four golfers and a few sponsors pull off our First Annual Crystal Rodriguez Golf Tournament. We raised enough money to give two $1,500 scholarships. Each year, the number of players and sponsors grows. The word got out that our tournament was not only for a good cause, but it is a fun one too. Of course, it helped that we moved the tournament to early October when it's not as cold! And for the first time, in October 2020, we filled the whole golf course with 144 players! Then, in 2021, we celebrated our 10th anniversary where we not only filled the course again, but we had the most sponsors that we ever had before. CRMSF conducts not only the golf tournament, but also a Crystal Ball throughout the year to raise money to distribute in scholarships.

The first and foremost goal of our 501(c)(3) not-for-profit organization is to provide partial scholarships to those applicants who exhibit high scholastic achievement, participate in school extracurricular activities, commit to community involvement, and have a good work ethic. We also put an emphasis on student financial need as an important component of our scholarship selection criteria.

Crystal was known for her passion for learning, sports, family, friends, and her faith in God. Her love for life left an impression on so many people who cared for her and loved her. It is the hope of the committee members that the winners of the scholarship will follow Crystal's example and use their talents and energy to actively make this world a better place to live.

It is our hope that we will continue to increase the number of scholarships awarded each year. We awarded two scholarships our first year and as of 2022 we've awarded seventy-seven scholarships...that's over $115,000 to deserving students!

You can learn more about The Crystal Rodriguez Memorial Scholarship Fund by visiting www.CRMSF2.com or email me at: Jeanfrodriguez@comcast.net.

100% of the proceeds of this book will be going to The Crystal Rodriguez Memorial Scholarship Fund.

Chapter Twenty-three

BEAUTY FOR ASHES
The Next Chapter

... To give them a crown of beauty for ashes, the oil of joy for mourning, and a garment of praise in place of a spirit of despair. So, they will be called oaks of righteousness, the planting of the LORD, that He may be glorified.

Isaiah 61:3[57]

SINCE THE TIME MY sons were young, I would pray for their future wives. I would pray that they would love Jesus and my sons, that they would have a deep respect for my boys and a love for life and a deep joy within them. These are just some of the prayers I would lift up. My prayers would change through the years, but no matter what I prayed, I always asked the Lord that whoever they married that they'd like me. I know, as a wife myself, the importance of liking the mother-in-law!

After Crystal died, Victor would tell me that he'd never be able to love again and that he would never get married a second time. I listened and completely understood his feelings, but I hoped for more.

Over three years had passed since Crystal's death, and one morning, as I was praying for family and friends, I sensed the Lord telling me that it was time to pray for Victor again, that he was not meant to be alone. In some ways, my prayers were the same as before: that she would love Jesus, that she would love and respect my son, and that she would have a love for life and a deep joy within her. But I knew that she had to be special to marry a widower. So, I prayed that the Lord would bring along someone who was compassionate, courageous, and confident in who she is, and that she would always be secure in Victor's love for her and our love for her. And, of course, I prayed that she would like me.

Over a year later, I was having lunch with Victor when he said, "Don't get excited, but I met a girl." Of course, I was thrilled and had a million questions. He told me that her name was Bailey and that she worked for the San Francisco Junior Giants Program. At that time, Victor worked at the Sunrise Park and Recreation District and Bailey was starting the Junior Giants program in Citrus Heights. Victor shared how Bailey came down from San Francisco a couple of times for meetings and that he blew them off and sent his friend and co-worker Troy Spivey instead. Troy would come back and report that Bailey was really cute, and he should meet her. On September 16, 2015, Bailey invited those who were involved in the Junior Giants to a Giants game. They all gathered in the right field of AT&T Park, and that is where Victor first met Bailey.

Of course, I did what every mom would do . . . I turned to social media to check her out! Fortunately for me, she had a public setting, so I was able to see her pictures and what she posted. I could see right away why Victor was so attracted to her; she was a beautiful young lady with a great smile, her posts were uplifting and incredibly positive, and she had a heart that was focused on others. I'm always so touched when a young person gets involved in helping others.

It was not long after he met Bailey that Victor received a job offer and he left his Park and Recreation job. Shortly thereafter, they went on their first date. They weren't dating long when Victor wanted us to meet her. It was a wonderful evening and she won us over with her graciousness and charm.

Over the coming months, they would travel back and forth from Sacramento to San Francisco visiting each other. Depending on traffic, it could take anywhere from two to three hours one way and that was taking a toll on Victor, and I'm sure Bailey, too. It seemed all of a sudden, Victor had a job opportunity to move to South San Francisco. I remember him telling me that he needed to live closer to Bailey so that they could see each other more often and so he moved to the Bay Area.

A little less than eighteen months later, Victor told me that he was going to ask Bailey to marry him. He decided he was going to propose in the same spot where he first met her, the right field of AT&T Park. He also planned a surprise engagement party afterward. She was completely shocked to discover the engagement party included not only both families and nearby friends, but Victor got ahold of her close sorority sisters from the University of California, Los Angeles (UCLA) and they all flew in for this special occasion. There were so many tears of joy that night, celebrating the love they had found in each other. Bailey put the sparkle back into Victor's eyes and it filled my heart with joy.

July 7, 2018, was the big day! Fifteen months after Victor proposed, friends and family from all over the country came to celebrate the wedding of Victor and Bailey. The day was exhilarating, and I was so excited to be a part of it all! We started the day with hair and makeup and lots of joy and laughter. It was Bailey, her mom Kathie, me, and all her best friends. It was really a beautiful and special time together.

Victor and Bailey decided to get their pictures taken before the wedding so that they could capture and remember their "first look." They shared that moment, just the two of them, but apparently Victor was so overwhelmed when he saw Bailey that he cried. It was a special time, an intimate time. They talked, prayed, and just enjoyed the moments together before all of the fun began.

It was an outdoor wedding, and they chose the perfect location—Shadelands Ranch in Walnut Creek. The stately shade trees towered above the lawn, gardens, and terrace. The sycamores and redwoods shaded the property and growing among them were citrus, pomegranate, and walnut trees with herb and vegetable gardens along the edges. Providing a charming backdrop was a beautifully restored 1903 Colonial revival house with curved glass bay windows that complemented the classical white columns and wraparound veranda. It was simply stunning.

They had their good friend Alejandro Vidal officiate the wedding. He opened our time together saying,

> *On behalf of the Rodriguez and West families, I'd like to thank you all for joining together as we witness what God has done in the lives of Victor and Bailey. In this moment, I would like to ask you to do something a little unordinary in 2018. I challenge you to be present. Allow the beauty of this moment to wash over you, admire the details of this day and who you get to spend it with. Give your pretty little phone camera a break; it deserves it and allow the Instagram worthy moments to be captured by the photographers.*

And with that, the wedding began. First, Victor walked down the aisle and turned to eagerly await his soon-to-be bride. Rubén and I followed. Then Bailey's brother Logan walked his mom Kathie down the aisle and then came the groomsmen and the bridesmaids. Everyone was in place waiting for the bride to make her entrance.

The music began and everybody rose to see Dan, Bailey's father, walk her down the aisle. She was simply radiant. As she made her way toward Victor, Bailey's maid of honor sang a gorgeous rendition of "Moon River." And when I saw Bailey, I couldn't help but turn to see Victor in all his anticipation. He had tears in his eyes as he watched his stunning bride come toward him.

As Bailey and her father reached the end of the aisle, Alejandro reminded us how all weddings give thanks for the past, celebrate the present, and honor the future. That it is an affirmation of who the couple is at this moment, as well as who they want to become, individually and as a couple. It is both that simple and that profound. Then Alejandro asked, "Who gives this woman to this man?" and Bailey's father said, "Her mother and I." He then kissed his daughter and presented her to Victor.

Alejandro continued,

> *In acknowledgement of this holy moment, let us bow our heads and pray. Jesus, we thank You so much for the miracle of marriage. We thank You for allowing these two souls to find each other at exactly the right time. We thank You for the journey that they are ready to embark upon with You being their guide. We thank You for their willingness to participate in the wonder of two hearts, two lives, and two souls becoming one. I ask that You fill their hearts with the reckless, steadfast, and never-ending love that You have for them. And that You would use this union to allow people to experience that love until the end of time. In Jesus' name, Amen.*

Everyone sat and Alejandro started the ceremony by saying,

> *Today is a sacred moment for so many reasons. Today, Victor and Bailey are telling the world that they choose each other over any other. They are professing to God and witnesses that they can do more for Jesus together than they could ever do apart. They are choosing to relinquish control of their individual dreams, ambitions, and desires to one another . . . To let those individual pieces of themselves be chiseled into a new masterpiece . . . A masterpiece that they will work together to create. Two families are being brought together today and an entirely new family is being created. That is the miracle of marriage.*
>
> *But how in the world did we get here? Anyone that has spent more than ten minutes with Victor knows that he is Sac town boy through and through. If you give him a chance, he will do his best to convince you that the Kings are soon-to-be basketball royalty, the next tech boom is going to erupt on the steps of the state capitol, and if you want to raise intelligent, vibrant, passionate, world-changing children, then you need to have a zip code that starts with a 956 something.*

Then you have Bailey who is one of the most independent, caring, driven women this side of heaven. I have known Bailey for almost a decade, and I have seen her gracefully transition through many phases of life. I have seen the "All I need in my life is Jesus and my girls" phase. I have seen the "All I need in my life is Jesus, my girls and a man" phase. Then the "Jesus, my girls and I ain't ever gonna need no man" phase. And finally arriving at this moment where she has found the one for whom her heart longs. Bailey has always been one to focus intently on what she wants and when she finds it, she pursues it relentlessly. To further illustrate this innate tenacity, she would like to read a letter that she wrote describing all the characteristics that her husband needed to have . . . she wrote this when she was twelve years old.

Bailey then proceeded to read from her little girl journal,

My perfect guy . . . who is he? I don't know who, but I think I know what. First of all, he has to be a Christian and have a genuine love for Jesus like me. He must be really funny and have a good sense of humor but can't be putting people down in the process. He has to also be smart, well maybe not as smart as me, but at least average (higher than average, I mean!). He has to like having tons of fun, like rollercoasters. Even if he's afraid to go on one, he must act like he's the strongest and bravest guy ever to me. He has to like dogs and other animals and be okay with them. He has to like basketball and baseball, but he can't be obsessed with either one. He must be athletic and good at sports. He also has to be cute . . . hot . . . handsome or whatever you want to call it. He has to be kind and under-standing. He must like the idea of an outdoor wedding, even if we don't do it. He must love me for me and not want me to change myself for his liking. He shouldn't have any tattoos or earrings, but the latter can always be fixed. He cannot smoke and can't drink too often. He has to support me in whatever

I want to do. Even if I want to be a makeup artist, he'll have to let me do makeup on him after his work. He has to have a good job. He can't complain if I say that someone else, like a baseball player, is cute. He'll already know that he's the real cute one. He must not be feminine. He has to like coffee, but not a lot, because it's kind of feminine. He has to let me pick the music in the car, and we have to have a convertible. He'll let me pick the kids' names. I know it sounds like I'm expecting a lot, but am I really? Well, okay, so it is a lot. So, what? That's okay. He's out there somewhere. Now I just have to find him.

Alejandro picked up right where Bailey left off.

After a few months with Victor, Bailey knew she found him. The way they met perfectly encapsulates the way millennials pursue love in 2018. A friend told Victor that he should check out a cutie that stopped by work a day that he wasn't there. He affectionately scoured the land of Facebook to do some stalking . . . I mean research and asked her to be his Facebook friend. Bailey accepted the request and then proceeded to start a conversation. They met in San Francisco, hit it off and, in the words of the poet/philosopher Drake, it went 0–100 really quick. Victor packed up, left his established life behind to pursue Bailey, and they discovered a love that has forever changed them.

Alejandro turned to Victor and Bailey and said,

The fact that you both are standing here today, hand in hand, is one of the clearest signs of God's love and care for you both. Victor, you once said to Bailey that you were blessed to have a great love story once and if you never had that again you'd be okay. You stood on the truth that God is good, all the time, even in the face of great tragedy. Regardless of your circumstance, you knew that God said in His Word that He has a plan for you, plans for welfare and not for evil. He says that

He will never leave you or forsake you, that no weapon formed against you shall prosper, and that you serve a God that gives good gifts to His children. Bailey is that gift.

Bailey, Victor was sent to you in a time where you didn't know if you'd ever find a love that could be put to the test. A time when you didn't think you would find a man that would do all that it took to encourage you, challenge you, and support you through any and all things. Victor is a gift from God to you. You both together are a testimony to us all that God is a redeemer of broken things. And how recklessly He loves you both.

He then continued,

Marriage was designed to focus on this love. Ravi Zacharias breaks it down so well. In English there is one word for love but in Greek there are four: agape (which is God's love), eros (romantic love), philia (which is the love for a friend), and storge (which is parental or protective love). Marriage is the only thing that brings these four together and is the most sacred relationship you will ever enter. In your marriage the task is simple, love God then love each other. Love each other with a love that is patient and kind, keeping no record of wrongs. Love each other tenaciously. A love that will not be separated by death nor life, present nor the future, nor any powers, neither height nor depth, nor anything else in all creation. Love each other the way Christ has loved you, in that He was willing to lay His life down for you so that you could have life and life everlasting. Above all, love each other because love covers a multitude of sins.

Alejandro went on to say,

As you both prepare to say your vows, I want you to look down at the hands you're holding. These are the hands of your best friend. The hands of the one that fully knows you and fully loves you. The hands that will hold you from the days of your youth to the days when wrinkles set in. These hands are those of your biggest fan, the hands that God is going to use to help you become who you were designed to be.

He then had Bailey and Victor take the following vows: "*I, Bailey, take you Victor, to be my husband, to have and to hold from this day forward, for better, for worse, for richer, for poorer, in sickness and in health, to love and to cherish, 'til death do us part, according to God's holy law, in the presence of God I make this vow.*"

Then he turned to Victor and asked him to repeat these words, "*I, Victor, take you, Bailey, to be my wife, to have and to hold from this day forward, for better, for worse, for richer, for poorer, in sickness and in health, to love and to cherish, 'til death do us part, according to God's holy law, in the presence of God I make this vow.*"

He asked for the rings and said, "*These rings are to serve as a constant reminder that you belong to one another; and that your love for each other is eternal.*"

Alejandro told the guests that for their first act as a married couple, Bailey and Victor would participate in communion. Then he read, "*The Lord Jesus, on the night he was betrayed, took bread, and when he had given thanks, he broke it and said, 'This is my body, which is for you; do this in remembrance of me.' In the same way, after supper he took the cup, saying, 'This cup is the new covenant in my blood; do this, whenever you drink it, in remembrance of me.*'[58] Christians do this to remember the sacrifice that Jesus made on the cross and to reflect on how they can be more like Jesus and engage in fellowship with God.*" Victor and Bailey then proceeded to take their first communion as a couple.

After communion, Alejandro said,

For as much as Victor and Bailey have promised to be faithful and true, each to the other, and have witnessed the same before God and this company by giving and receiving a ring and by

*joining hands; now, therefore, by virtue of the authority vested
in me by God and the State of California, I now pronounce
you husband and wife. Those whom God had joined together
let no one attempt to separate. You may kiss your bride.*

The maid of honor than returned the bridal bouquet to Bailey and
both Victor and Bailey turned and looked at the crowd as Alejandro
said this benediction: *"Now to Him who is able to keep you from falling,
and to make you stand without blemish in the presence of His glory with
rejoicing, to the only God our Savior, through Jesus Christ our Lord,
be glory, majesty, power, and authority, before all time and now and
forever. Amen."*[59]

He then said, *"Ladies and Gentlemen, I now present to you for the
first time Mr. and Mrs. Victor and Bailey Rodriguez!!"*

The celebration continued onto the expansive lawn at the back
of the house. During cocktail hour, the photographer took pictures
of the families and friends, the guests mingled, playing lawn games
and sipping on various signature drinks. When it was time, the guests
found their seats and waited for the bridal party to be introduced and
for the grand entrance of bride and groom. Accompanied by cheers and
hoots and hollers, Victor and Bailey made their way to their private
table under a gazebo encircled by roses.

When it was time for dinner, we had a choice of two food trucks,
everything from sliders to lobster rolls. As we ate, Bailey's three maids
of honor , Makayla Hamilton, Jaclyn Morimune, and Ashley Cordero
along with Victor's three best men, Kevin Lindner, Kevin Halfhill, and
Shane Karp, gave marvelous toasts that were incredibly endearing and
oh so funny at the same time. But, when her dad Dan went to give his
toast, he was so overwhelmed with emotions that he spent seventy-five
percent of his toast choking back tears.

As the evening went on, the tiny lights woven through the trees,
added an enchanting ambiance as night fell. It also added something
special to the most awaited moment for the bride and groom. With
great anticipation, we watched as Victor and Bailey stepped out to the

dance floor to have their first dance. They chose "Yours" by Russell Dickerson.[60] As they danced in celebration of their union, I just had to smile to see my son, once again, in love. All eyes were on them, and they only had eyes for each other.

I just loved the chorus of the song:

I came to life when I first kissed you
The best me has his arms around you
You make me better than I was before
Thank God I'm yours

As the song finished, Victor stepped aside for Dan to dance with his daughter. Knowing the relationship that Bailey has with her dad, I realized that "Father and Daughter" by Paul Simon truly was the perfect song.[61] The chorus says it all:

I'm gonna watch you shine
Gonna watch you grow
Gonna paint a sign
So you always know
As long as one and one is two
There could never be a father
Love his daughter more than I love you!

Then it was my turn to dance with my boy! He picked the song, "The Perfect Fan" by the Backstreet Boys.[62] I had a permanent smile on my face and I'm pretty sure I looked like a Cheshire cat, I was so happy. I was simply delighted that Victor found someone to love and who loved him. At one point, Victor said, "Listen to the words of the song." And I heard:

You showed me when I was young just how to grow
You showed me everything I should know
You showed me just how to walk without your hands
'Cuz Mom you always were the perfect fan.

Then it was time for the party to begin as the DJ opened the dance floor with "The Middle" by Zedd and Maren Morris.[63] The dance floor was full the whole evening and you could see the bride and groom's excitement as they danced with their best friends and family. I don't think they left the dance floor all night.

Sadly, the evening had to come to an end. We lined both sides of the walkway with our three-foot sparklers in hand and Victor and Bailey came running through as the light shone upon them.

EPILOGUE

You have turned my mourning into joyful dancing. You have taken away my clothes of mourning and clothed me with joy, that I might sing praises to you and not be silent. O Lord my God, I will give you thanks forever!

Psalm 30:11–12[64]

A LITTLE MORE THAN two years after their marriage, Victor and Bailey had a healthy and beautiful baby boy named Quinn West Rodriguez. He was born on the day that we had the Ninth Annual Crystal Rodriguez Memorial Golf Tournament. He has a cool birth-date: 10–10–20 and weighed seven pounds and seven ounces. He is the first grandchild on both sides of the family, and we were so thrilled welcoming him into the world!

Six months later, Victor, Bailey, Quinn and their two dogs, Piper and Cooper, moved to Rocklin, California, which is only a fifteen-minute drive from our house. It is a new season in our life, and we are taking it in and enjoying every moment!

AFTERWORD

THERE IS ONE MORE thing that I wanted to share with you . . . that thing is that God has always LOVED you and *He* wants *you* to experience the peace and life He has to offer! Throughout this book, you've learned all about our freedom to choose and how God has given us the choice.

We have freedom to choose . . .

> To trust rather than fear.
>
> To not let anger rule.
>
> To not let your wounds make you someone you don't want to be.

There's freedom to choose hope over despair.
But most of all, you have the freedom to choose Jesus as your Lord and Savior.

My question to you is: Have you made that choice?

If you haven't asked Jesus to have a personal relationship with you, and that's your desire, you can start now. And that decision has an eternal impact!

If you're all in but you don't know what to say, here's a prayer for you:

> Father, I recognize that I am a sinner and I need a Savior.
> I believe Jesus is your Son. I believe that He died for me
> and rose again. Jesus, I open my heart to You, and I accept
> You as my Lord and Savior. I want to follow You and love
> You. Please fill me with your Holy Spirit and help me to be
> more like You.
>
> In Jesus' name,
> Amen.

If you just prayed this prayer, you may want to jot down your initials and today's date next to the prayer. These will serve as reminders of the day you chose a personal relationship with Jesus Christ, trusting Him as your Lord and Savior.

And because God forgives us, we seek to forgive others. One of the greatest things you can do once you've started your journey with Jesus is to forgive those who've wronged you. For help in seeking forgiveness, restoration, and healing in your life, go to: https://newsletters.crosswalk.com/direct-cw-prayers-for-forgiveness/ and download the FREE prayer guide on forgiveness.

ACKNOWLEDGEMENTS

Rubén—To my amazing husband, we walked this journey together, side by side, and I couldn't have done it without you!

Kevin—To my eldest son, who, because of Crystal's death, struggled with his faith but in the end, came out standing firm.

Manny Rodriguez—Thank you for dropping everything and flying down to the Bahamas to stand by our side to give us moral support.

Eddie and Maria Rodriguez—We will never forget, and are forever grateful, that you opened your home and let us stay over a month while Victor was in the ICU.

Mary Karp—What would I have done without you? You were there when I needed you most and I will never forget that. I am blessed to have you as my sister!!

Cathy Haviland—Thank you for flying down to Los Angeles so that Kevin didn't have to fly home alone.

Calendar Girls (My Thursday Bible study lifeline)—Debbie Bernard, Sharon Bluemel, Leota Burlin, Suzanne Delfin, Penny Doane, Cathy Haviland, Shirley Hoffman, Suzanne Papamichail and Mary Leigh Scherer. Thank you for being there in our family's darkest hour. For all your love, your tender words and for just letting me cry. I give thanks for your friendship, love, and support.

Beauties (My Friday Bible Study Crew)—Mary Boies, Diane Ciraulo, Linda Earls, Pam Hill, Joanna Larrew, Theresa Maloney, Julie Morton, Kim Paine, Sharon Russo, and Darlene Takegami. Thank you for all your prayers, comforting words, and your emotional support.

Joanna Larrew—Thank you for your insight, asking tough questions, and your words of comfort and wisdom.

Tori Wible—Thank you for capturing Victor and Crystal's last memories through the beautiful pictures you took at their wedding, and for being my friend.

Valley Springs Presbyterian Church—Thank you for opening your church so that Victor and Crystal had a place to get married.

Nancy DeGlymes—Thank you for providing the calla lilies and for making the foyer in the church look gorgeous for the wedding.

Karen and Jenn Check—Thank you for making a way for me to have some time alone. The cabin at Mount Hermon was the perfect place to spend time with the Lord.

Bailey—Thank you for putting the sparkle back into my son's eyes.

Past* and Present Board Members of The Crystal Rodriguez Memorial Scholarship Fund (CRMSF): Victor & Bailey Rodriguez, Rubén & Jeanne Rodriguez, Troy & Sarah Spivey, Brian Schweppe, Kevin Lindner, Vance Charvo, Lisa Lindner, Chris Andrews*, Dolly Whitfield*, Tim Carroll*—Thank you for the countless hours you have put in to make the golf tournaments and the Crystal Ball to be successful fundraisers.

A special thank you for all who came to visit Victor while he was in the hospital in Florida, when he was so far away from home: Jackie and Ross Bachelor, Yvonne, Richie, and Mateo Gonzalez, Mary Karp, Josh Roome, and Eileen and Pat Orgen and their four beautiful girls.

To our church family at Bayside Church of Granite Bay, all my family, friends and the local community who prayed for us, provided meals and who donated their time and money to the fundraisers. You will always have a special place in my heart!

Dave Eaton—Thank you for the beautiful cover you designed for my book. It is a work of art!

Emily Wheatley—I am deeply indebted for your editorial assistance. You made me a better writer and I couldn't have done it without you.

Rhonda Elfstrand—Thank you, my friend, you put the final touches by proofreading the book.

ENDNOTES

1   Author Unknown

2   Taken from Airman's Odyssey by Antoine de Saint-Exupery © 1939. Used by permission of Harcourt Brace & Company, New York.

3   Music Video by Alison Krauss. © 1995 Rounder Records. Manufactured and distributed by Concord Music Group, Inc.

4   Celine Dion, Falling into You Album, released February 20, 1996, Sony Music Entertainment (Canada) Inc.

5   Louis Armstrong, What a Wonderful World Album, released September 1, 1967, ABC

6   Revelation 2:10b King James Version (KJV)

7   Taken from *A Grace Disguised* (How the Soul Grows Through Loss) by Jerry Sittser © 2004. Used by permission of Zondervan, Grand Rapids, Michigan.

8   Deuteronomy 31:6b

9   Taken from *Jesus Calling: Enjoying Peace in His Presence* by Sarah Young © 2004 by Sarah Young. Used by permission of Thomas Nelson. www.thomasnelson.com

10   Taken from *Smile Anyway: Quotes, Verse, and Grumblings for Every Day of the Year*, by Richelle E. Goodrich, © 2015. Used by permission of CreateSpace Independent Publishing Platform.

11   Bird in Tree (sent to me as a comment in a newspaper article)

12   Taken from *Jesus Calling: Enjoying Peace in His Presence* by Sarah Young © 2004 by Sarah Young. Used by permission of Thomas Nelson. www.thomasnelson.com

13   Used by permission of Sebastian Thrun

14   Isaiah 41:10

15   Psalm 56:8 New Living Translation (NLT)

16   Taken from *A Grace Disguised* (How the Soul Grows Through Loss) by Jerry Sittser © 2004. Used by permission of Zondervan, Grand Rapids, Michigan.

17   Matthew 20:21

18   Matthew 20:32

19   Luke 24:38

20   Used by permission of Robert J. Morgan

21   Nahum 1:3 New Living Translation (NLT)

22   Nahum 1:7 New Living Translation (NLT)

23   Deuteronomy 29:29a

24   *A Grief Observed*, C. S. Lewis, Publisher: Faber and Faber, United Kingdom, © 1961

25   John 16:22

26   "Homesick", Mercy Me, Undone Album, released April 20, 2004, by INO Records.

27   Psalm 23, New King James Version (NKJV)

28   Revelation 21:1–5, New King James Version (NKJV)

29   "Homesick", Mercy Me, Undone Album, released April 20, 2004, by INO Records.

30   Romans 15:13, New King James Version (NKJV)

31   Psalm 116:1

32   Psalm 116:15

33   Taken from *Out of Solitude: Three Meditations on the Christian Life*, Chapter 15, by Henri Nouwen, © 2004. Used by permission of Ave Maria Press Book.

34   Psalm 34:18

35   "Hold My Heart", Tenth Avenue North, Album, released on May 20, 2008, by Over and Underneath Studio.

36   Proverbs 3:5

37   Joni Erickson Tada, Used by permission

38   Psalm 143:1

39   Romans 8:31

40   *Saying Goodbye* © 2017 by Zoe Clark-Coates. Used by permission of David C. Cook. May not be further reproduced. All rights reserved.

41   This quote has been credited to Ralph Waldo Emerson, Oliver Wendell Holmes, Jr., and Henry David Thoreau

42   Psalm 138:7, English Standard Version (ESV)

43   Psalm 138:8, English Standard Version (ESV)

44   Psalm 139:2

45   Job 17:11, New Living Translation (NLT)

46   Desmond Tutu, used by permission of Tutu Foundation UK.

47   Romans 5:5a, New King James Version (NKJV)

48   Romans 15:13

49   Romans 5:5, New King James Version (NKJV)

50   Isaiah 49:23b

51   Job 17:11, New Living Translation (NLT)

52   Psalm 39:7

53   Psalm 62:5

54   Titus 1:2

55   Used by permission of Steve Maraboli

56   Author Unknown

57   Isaiah 61:3

58   1 Corinthians 11:24–25

59   Jude 24–25, New Revised Standard Version (NRSV)

60   Russell Dickerson, Yours Album, released July 23, 2015, independently to digital retailers and online streaming services.

61   Wild Thornberry's movie soundtrack, released December 1, 2013

62   Backstreet Boys, Millennium released on May 18, 1999, by Jive Records.

63   Zedd, Maren Morris, "The Middle," released on January 23, 2018, by Interscope Records.

64   Psalm 30:11–12 New Living Translation (NLT)